THE MUMMY

TOMB OF THE DRAGON EMPEROR

THE MUMMY

TOMB OF THE DRAGON EMPEROR

Introduction by Rob Cohen

A NEWMARKET PICTORIAL MOVIEBOOK

Designed by Timothy Shaner, nightanddaydesign.biz

FIRST EDITION

10 9 8 7 6 5 4 3 2 1   10 9 8 7 6 5 4 3 2 1
ISBN: 978-1-55704-805-9 (paperback)   ISBN: 978-1-55704-806-6 (hardcover)

Library of Congress Catalog-in-Publication Data available upon request.

QUANTITY PURCHASES
Companies, professional groups, clubs, and other organizations may qualify for special terms
when ordering quantities of this title. For information, write to Special Sales, Newmarket
Press, 18 East 48th Street, New York, NY 10017; call (212) 832-3575 or 1-800-669-3903;
FAX (212) 832-3629; or e-mail info@newmarketpress.com.

www.newmarketpress.com

Manufactured in the United States of America.

Other Newmarket Pictorial Moviebooks include:

The Art of The Matrix*
The Art of X2*
The Art of X-Men: The Last Stand
Bram Stoker's Dracula: The Film and the Legend*
Chicago: The Movie and Lyrics*
Dances with Wolves: The Illustrated Story of the Epic Film*
Dreamgirls
E.T. The Extra-Terrestrial: From Concept to Classic*
Gladiator: The Making of the Ridley Scott Epic Film

Memoirs of a Geisha: A Portrait of the Film
The Namesake: A Portrait of the Film by Mira Nair
Ray: A Tribute to the Movie, the Music, and the Man*
Rescue Me: Uncensored
Rush Hour 1, 2, 3: Lights, Camera, Action!
Saving Private Ryan: The Men, The Mission, The Movie
Schindler's List: Images of the Steven Spielberg Film
Superbad: The Illustrated Moviebook*
Tim Burton's Corpse Bride: An Invitation to the Wedding

Includes screenplay.

Contents

Introduction
Connecting to The Mummy
By Rob Cohen

In the fall of 2001, Stacy Snider, then head of production at Universal, hosted an evening to introduce her new slate of films to a conclave of Universal distribution executives and film buyers from across the country. Two directors were invited to present their films. I was there for *The Fast and the Furious* and Stephen Sommers was showing some footage from *The Mummy Returns*. Stephen is a charming, gregarious guy who loves yoga, pilates, taking his young equestrian daughters to their hunter/jumper competitions, and making big-scale, big-hit commercial movies.

That night, both of our presentations went extremely well and we were in a high, confident mood, a rare feeling in Hollywood. We shared the bonhomie that movie directors can only feel when prospects are equally bright for all present (as we are often in competition with one another to land a film the studios want to make). It was a great night and Stephen and I promised to stay in touch, have lunch—you know, the usual. I was not to see him again for five years.

Flash forward to the autumn of 2006. My wonderful William Morris agents Jim Wiatt and Rob Carlson called to say they wanted me to look at the script of *Mummy 3*, as it was then known. Stephen Sommers, his partner Bob Ducsay, and producer

Opposite: Concept drawing of the terra-cotta head of Jet Li by the Aaron Sims Company. Right: Director Rob Cohen standing amid the terra-cotta warriors created for the movie.

Sean Daniel had asked if I'd be remotely interested in the project; they were looking for a director.

I'd seen *The Mummy Returns* and had no idea where a third movie could go with the same elements. That's when Carlson said one simple sentence that changed everything: "It takes place in China and the mummies are the Terracotta Army of Xi'an!"

"Send me the script right away," I said. An hour later, the script arrived by messenger.

Why was I so intrigued? First and foremost, I have a deep love of Chinese culture and a complete fascination with the sweep and tumult of its 5,000-year history. Since high school, when my mother began painting Chinese watercolors as a hobby, China had occupied my imagination and reading time. I was intrigued by various dynasties, most especially the Tang and the Ming with their early explorers discovering Indonesia, India, Africa, and the giant "treasure ships" that may have circumvented the world long before Magellan, and might have reached the Americas long before Columbus.

I was delighted by the rise of the "Fifth Generation" film directors and the sumptuous works they produced, such as *Red Sorghum*, *Raise the Red Lantern*, *Ju Dou*, *Yellow Earth*, *Farewell My Concubine*, *To Live*, and more recent Chinese achievements, *Hero* and *House of Flying Daggers*. Directors such as Zhang Yimou and Chen Kaige, and actresses such as Gung Li, put magnificent images to the stories I'd read as a child. In the 60s, I'd participated in the anti–Vietnam War movement, read Mao's "Little Red Book," and flirted with his communal social visions. Later, I traveled twice to China to see the Great Wall, Beijing, and glamorous Shanghai. Ultimately, I lived in Hong Kong and Macau while making *Dragon: The Bruce Lee Story*—a very Chinese movie full of interracial love and blistering martial arts—working with a Chinese crew, eating the local food, wandering the markets and the neighborhoods on the

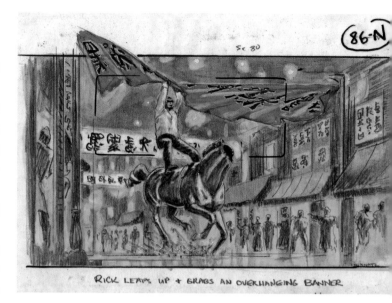

RICK LEAPS UP + GRABS AN OVERHANGING BANNER

Above: Storyboard panel by Nikita Knatz. Right: The Emperor's mystics inside the Foundation chamber. Above right: Storyboard panel by Patrick Desgreniers of the Ninghxia excavation site.

weekends, and absorbing the musicality of Cantonese. My son was five years old at the time and, just for fun, we used to ride the Star ferry back and forth across the harbor in Hong Kong. It is no small coincidence my son is now majoring in Chinese studies at Sarah Lawrence College, taking his junior year abroad at Fudan University in Shanghai. Such is the grip of China.

Still later in my life, I converted to Buddhism, a fundamental set of teachings that helped organize and unify Chinese culture for centuries. Buddhism brought me emotionally closer to the history I'd already absorbed and gave me a new way to understand and relate to the daily experience of "Chinese-ness," if there is such a word.

A few years ago, I bought a home in Bali where the mix of Hindu, Buddhism, and animism generates a sweetness in the people that I've yet to find anywhere else in the world. Getting to Bali requires a stop in Hong Kong, Singapore, Taiwan, or Bangkok so, over the years, I've had ample time to explore all of them and discover the ways in which each place has been connected to China.

Having lived among the explosive energy of Asia makes reading a Hollywood script about China a very different experience, something I felt after finishing *The Mummy 3* script by Al Gough and Miles Millar, two talented writers who'd created *Smallville* and written many features, from *Shanghai Noon* to *Spiderman 2*.

Their script was engrossing, funny, and a speedy read.

I called Rob Carlson and said as much. We agreed I should meet with the producers to discuss the project. Rob also represents Stephen and Bob, and the agency reps Gough and Millar. Such is the way things happen in Hollywood: a cathexis of need develops and flows like several streams into a roaring river that either washes away all resistance or results in those same streams smashing against each other. One never knows at the start. You just have to take the plunge.

Our first meeting took place in the offices of Steve Sommers and Bob Ducsay, above the Coffee Bean on the Third Street Promenade, where Steve, Bob, and Sean Daniel were waiting for me in a suite filled with posters and artifacts from their films.

These meetings can be likened to a forward scout tip-toeing through a minefield. Every script developed through the studio system comes with a long history of original inspiration, conflicting visions, and compromise. A director coming into the mix has no idea who is devoted to which ideas and no sense of the sometimes bitter arguments that have ensued in arriving at this 120-page blueprint for a dream or, more accurately perhaps, a dream of a dream. The art of these meetings—and it *is* an art—is to separate the "pick-up sticks," one from the other, until some of the fissures lying beneath the surface are revealed. Even with

true gentlemen like these three accomplished producers, there are secrets and sensitivities to probe.

The script had the tone and intention of the first two movies—which would be the natural point of departure for developing any sequel; it clearly captured the iconic characters and contained a good deal of invention. But the danger of creating the third installment along such familiar lines is an ineffable fatigue woven into the material, the "been there, done that" factor, no matter how inventive. Also, the audience, the zeitgeist, had shifted in the intervening five years since *The Mummy Returns*.

However, I was completely hooked by the idea of setting the film in China and using the terra-cotta warriors

From left to right: Producer Bob Ducsay, director Rob Cohen, producer Sean Daniel, and executive producer Chris Brigham.

of Xi'an. I understood the incredible potential of such a concept. I got it. Nothing else mattered.

Fueled by this mutual core of agreement, the two-hour meeting with Bob, Sean, and Steve rolled on as if we were all old friends (which is true for Sean Daniel, a friend I've known for 30 years). Steve was gregarious and open about his thoughts, and had little proprietary protection of the material, which was refreshing. No one was attacking; no one was defending. There was a lot of laughter, too much coffee, and I left feeling that this was a group with whom I could work well. Since that is rarely the case, it was not to be minimized in my final decision about whether or not to take on this project.

By Friday, I was sitting around a long conference table with Bob, Sean, and the upper management of Universal—chairman Marc Shmuger, co-chair David Linde, president

Above: Rob Cohen directing an early morning crew meeting. Photo by John Platt. Below: Producers Sean Daniel and Stephen Sommers.

Donna Langley, senior vice-president Jeff Kirschenbaum, and director of development Erik Baiers. I have a long history with Universal: I produced my first film for them in 1975. In fact, of the 30 movies I've produced or directed, half of them were for this one studio. Marc Shmuger was the head of marketing when I made *The Fast and the Furious* and it was his decision to take my film out of the spring-break slot and move it into the summer between *A.I.* and *Tomb Raider*, a decision that was deemed suicidal by many—at least until *Fast* beat both on the weekend charts and gave birth to two sequels, video games, arcade games, triple-platinum albums, and such.

Marc was as insightful and thoughtful as any executive I'd ever met. I knew he liked the truth and sensed he was searching for a way to make this sequel *Mummy* fresh. I told them my approach.

The script, I explained, played fast and loose with history. It did not take the time to honor the Chinese culture and felt glib in these respects. I'd already discussed this with Al Gough and Miles Millar, the writers, and they agreed we needed to deepen the grandeur and vision of this period setting.

The script had a vague focus beyond the coolest idea ever (that the terra-cotta army were the mummies). I wanted to intensify the father/son story and develop the "old bull/young bull" aspects that were only implied in the draft. To make this most effective, I wanted to raise Alex's age from 17 to 21, to heighten that moment when the father is finally forced to deal with the son as an equal, to see him as the man he has become, not the child he once was. (Later, we named our production company "Old Bull/Young Bull Productions.")

I stressed the need to shoot all exteriors in China, to feel the geography and the very earth of China, to make it a co-star in the story. I foresaw an entire Chinese art department with historical and military experts helping us get everything very right.

I expressed two other strong feelings in the meeting,

Jet Li on set, standing before the lavishly detailed Emperor's map of his conquered lands.

the only absolute imperatives in rebooting the franchise: one was Brendan Fraser, an actor I'd admired since his powerful performance in Bill Condon's disturbing *Gods and Monsters*, an admiration that was further deepened by his memorable presence in Phillip Noyce's excellent *The Quiet American*. To my mind, there simply was no other Rick O'Connell. Brendan had created the role out of whole cloth and the suit fit only him.

The other idea was simple: in addition to Brendan Fraser and John Hannah, I wanted to have Jet Li play the emperor who gets cursed and baked alive in a shell of terra-cotta. He was a must.

I had talked for an hour straight, so it was time to get off stage and let them decide among themselves. I had presented some sweeping notions of change. Because a successful movie franchise is a studio's most valuable asset, a fundamental change of direction is not always welcome.

I was in bumper to bumper traffic on the 101 Freeway making my way back to my home in Malibu when Marc

Shmuger called. He relayed his and his cohorts' excitement about all the ideas. We had total creative agreement. Warmly, we wished each other Merry Christmas/Happy New Year and, digitally, we shook hands over the phone.

Thus, the third installment of *The Mummy* franchise was launched.

The Director and Production Designer Connection

At the core of a film lies a relationship, not often discussed, between the director and production designer. Much has been written about other binary units in filmmaking: director/writer, director/cameraman, director/editor, director/producer; but as I look around, I've yet to find a work that fully illuminates this critical relationship. Throughout my career, I've come to understand that the partnership between the production designer and director gives a film its textural and tonal integrity and positions it for all that will happen subsequently. Other players will place their hands on the Ouji board but, in the alliance between these two jobs, a movie generates its first stirrings of life.

Let me digress for a short historical overview. The title "production designer" replaced "art director" in 1939 as the most senior crew member in a film's art department. The title refers to the person designated to help create the overall look of films, television programs, music videos, and/or commercials. The first time it appeared on screen was on the 1939 epic *Gone With the Wind*, which was designed by the legendary William Cameron Menzies. David O. Selznick, the monolithic producer of the film, believed that Menzies's diverse contributions to the film were so far-reaching that the title "art director" was insufficient. Thus, a new name for "super" art directors burst on the screen and the indispensability and stature of these artists was properly credited at last.

The production designer job requires knowledge of art, architecture, photography, color, construction techniques, fashion trends, and the script. As a department head, executive abilities and leadership qualities are critical for the production designer to translate the director's vision into reality, balanced with financial resources. Many people could dream up a film's look, good or bad to some degree, but few can dream it and build it on a strict schedule and within budgetary limits.

There is further complexity in the job when it comes to taste. In the time it takes for a film to get from pre- to post-production, between one to three years, fashions change. Stylistic elements that are popular one season can fade to cliché in the next. The production designer, therefore, always faces the challenge of balancing the "hip" ephemeral elements of current fads and trends with classic cinema values. Like the director, the designer must find a way to mount a particular story that will be experienced by an audience years down the line—and then forever. Striking the proper chord and tone is the key to the enduring value of a film.

Finding Nigel

Every director does his prep differently, but long ago I learned from directors I had worked with and respected, like Tony Richardson (he was the first director on *Mahogany*, my first movie as a producer): *Everything stems from the design*. The sooner the design is in place, the sooner the other pieces of the massive movie puzzle can come together. There are a thousand ways into a movie, but selecting and working with the production designer always made the most sense to me.

For me, a movie is not only a visual experience; it also needs to be a physical experience that transcends the 2-D plane of your local cinema screen. In my films, I've tried to re-create physical sensations: the actual experience of speed in the four-car drag race in *The Fast and the Furious* and the adrenaline rush of the snowboard/avalanche sequence in *xXx,* to cite two examples. In order to create this connection

with the audience, the physical environment and tonal approach must be built from the script up, layer upon layer. To achieve this, I must invite into the film a person of vision, artistry, logistical understanding, and budgetary sensitivity. Sets, construction schedules, costs are only the half of it; the more important half is the discernment of my goals and the co-creation of the movie's tone.

After canvassing the availability of my favorite production designers, I narrowed my choice down to three, only one with whom I'd previously worked. I arranged meetings for Bob Ducsay and me to set out on the hunt: two at the Rose Café in Venice, and a later one in "the whale," the gaping conference room at Digital Domain. Over coffee with my past collaborator, I quickly realized it wasn't going to work. An Academy Award nomination had just arrived for her most recent achievement, and she was hopelessly overcommitted to family and other projects.

An hour later, in walked Nigel Phelps, wearing a John Lennon hat over his long pageboy hair. I was familiar with his tremendous work on Wolfgang Peterson's *Troy*, and two Michael Bay films: *Pearl Harbor* and *The Island*. These

Right: Production designer Nigel Phelps (left) with Rob Cohen.
Opposite: The ruined Great Wall set. Photograph by John Platt.

films all contained complex period designs, location builds, studio builds, and enormous imagination. Nigel seemed to have a real feeling for history and a lovely sense of space and texture.

Bob, Nigel, and I sat on high stools sipping our second or third round of caffeine. Thus wired, I launched into what I knew about the cultural aspect of mounting *Mummy 3*, the intriguing history of the story, and the differences I was striving to achieve in this new film from its hugely successful predecessors. I revealed my hopes to reboot the franchise in an action/adventure, *Raiders of the Lost Ark* tradition, with more realistic jeopardy and a greater reliance on the actual architecture of early-empire China.

Nigel talked of similar challenges he'd faced on *Troy*, specifically in dealing with that confluence where the research of the period confronted the long-nurtured mythology accepted by most people. "Blimey, those walls (of Troy) weren't really very high once you get right down to it!" Nigel exclaimed. "Maybe ten feet made of mud. That was the real challenge—how to show the history but not be devoured by it."

I fell in professional love from that moment. Nigel understood my challenge: how to capture the epic nature of second century B.C. China in an accurate way without being overwhelmed by the pursuit. I wanted my film to be grounded in reality, but it still had to be pitched to feature a three-headed dragon, the mythological yeti, and a terra-cotta army that comes back to life. Tonally blending

this into the live action part of the film would take great control and even greater skill.

At that meeting, Nigel and I talked about architecture, interior design, prop building, and my new main tenants: cultural accuracy and tremendous visual beauty. I left Nigel with the script, the research I'd already amassed, and the challenge of, among many other things, re-creating the terra-cotta army of Xi'an as it might have been when it was entombed 2,200 years ago. I saw the inner pilot lights fire in his brown eyes.

Still, he had not committed to the project. Like all talented people, he needed time to read and reflect. Signing on would be a one-year commitment to be in China and other locations outside of Los Angeles. Wives, children, and other obligations must be consulted and considered, as well as weighing other offers against mine. A day later, Nigel called to say he was in. The next day, I moved him into my production offices and we were off.

First Steps

There was little time to waste, but Nigel and I spent a good deal of time talking. We watched DVDs (which I highly recommend): *The Emperor and the Assassin*, *The Emperor's Shadow*, and, of course, *Hero*. Then we discussed the textures, sets, props, cinematography—what we liked and didn't like. These films clearly showed the schizophrenic attitude the Chinese maintain about their imperial past, even today. Reading book after book on the terra-cotta army of Xi'an, the cause was apparent: such grandeur of vision was so evenly countered by such cruelty.

There was another aspect of the design of this movie that is perhaps more true in action films than in other genres. In a drama, environments are used to set the stage for and reflect aspects of the characters that the director and production designer want the audience to visually perceive. In a film such as ours, the sets *are* characters. They move and supply threat; they create opportunities for physical interaction, just like any other actor.

In this film, several major builds would perform this function: the booby-trapped mausoleum containing the terra-cotta army, the cog room (the complex of water wheels), and the astrolabe set. These three sets would be built on stages and require enormous amounts of engineering. Almost all departments would be brought into play to make them work successfully, a great deal falling on the broad shoulders of special effects supervisor Bruce Steinheimer.

Building Our Team

From early in pre-production, the production designer influences key personnel in other departments, including the costume designer, the key hair and make-up stylists, the special effects director, and the locations manager (among others) to help the director establish a unified visual appearance to the film. While all the theory and history were flying around the production offices, Nigel and I were taking concrete steps along different lines. Nigel was hiring illustrators, art directors, draftsmen, sketch-up computer artists, and model makers.

The art department on a film works with the production designer to implement scenic elements. The art director supervises set construction and painting, as well as modifications to existing locations. On a film as complex as ours, for example, in Montreal I had one supervising art director (Isabelle Guay) working for the production designer and seven assistant art directors under her. Further down the pyramid are myriad specialists including construction foremen, carpenters, set painters, plasterers, structural engineers, computer technicians (for 3-D modeling), prop builders, model makers, greens-men (landscape experts), sign painters, and scenic artists (specialists in giving all sets the proper age and detail).

Before this army comes into play, a small group of production illustrators is hired to "visualize" the sets through sketches or paintings (mostly done on computers). These artists are very important to me as a director, both for helping me understand the ramifications of Nigel's and my musings and theories and for giving these speculative environments a sense of light. A good illustrator is a closet cameraman and bathes the conceptual painting in the most dramatic and mood-inducing light to show off the set in its most powerful potential.

While Nigel was building his department, I was hiring the all-important costume and creature designers. For costumes, my first choice was Sanja Hays, who could design the most outrageous clothes, say, for Russian hookers in *xXx* or street racer girls in *Fast*. I found her to be talented in the extreme (in all versions of that phrase) and a lovely person with whom to collaborate. Originally from Croatia,

From left: Action unit director Vic Armstrong, Rob Cohen, and producer James Jacks on the Oxfordshire fishing set. Opposite: Isabella Leong prepares for a scene on the Himalayas set, built in Montreal, Canada.

Sanja brings with her a vision of old-world craftsmanship, cultural understanding, and a complete love of her world. Actors, I knew from experience, love her, and getting *my* sense of the clothes to be *their* interpretation of the clothes is always a tightrope dance. She loved the potential of the Chinese story and embraced it totally.

Once Sanja was onboard, I set my sights on a creature designer. *The Mummy: Tomb of the Dragon Emperor* is populated by many fantastic creatures that would need to blend seamlessly with the historical story. I had Yeti coming to the rescue in the Himalayas and a terra-cotta version of the Emperor that needed the emotive presence of Jet Li. In addition, Jet's Emperor character is a shape-shifter who turns himself into a three-headed dragon and then a Nian, a huge temple guardian lion/dog (there are kitsch versions of them in front of many Chinese restaurants). We also needed to design hundreds of desiccated slaves who are resurrected from underneath the Great Wall to form the army that will battle the Emperor's reawakened terra-cotta troops in the climactic third act. This was a tall order in that, normally, each of these creatures would require six months to design; we didn't have six months to create all of them.

There was one artist I knew by reputation whose work had the right feel to bring into our team: Aaron Sims. He'd worked with legendary Rick Baker and, later, for the supremely talented Stan Winston (who'd been a young make-up genius on *The Wiz*, which I produced in 1978). Aaron had all the qualities expressed in his great work on *Men in Black, The Grinch, A.I.,* and others. He came to my office and, after ten minutes, I offered him the job, which he graciously accepted. We decided to start with the Yeti (our version of the Abominable Snowman), as both of us knew from past challenges that creating a living thing that does not exist in nature is truly difficult, bordering on impossible.

Now with the sets, the clothes, and the creatures being created, the next step for me was to find the person with whom I could work to capture and enhance the beauty I saw in my mind's eye, a person who could elevate and unify the vision with light: the cinematographer.

Searching for Simon

I've been blessed with many great cinematographers in my career. My first film, *Mahogany* (starring Diana Ross and Billy Dee Williams), was shot by David Watkin, who won an Academy Award for his work on *Out of Africa*. Vilmos Zsigmond shot *The Witches of Eastwick*, directed by George Miller, which I produced. Dean Semler, who won the golden statue for *Dances with Wolves*, shot both *xXx* and *Stealth*. It is impossible to describe or overemphasize their contributions to the success of these films.

I've also worked with young talent, newer to the field: Jeffrey Kimball (later of *Topgun* fame) on *The Legend of Billie Jean*, directed by my old friend Matthew Robbins; Ericson Core on *The Fast and the Furious*; and Shane Hurlbut on my films *The Rat Pack* and *The Skulls*. These men added a dimension to each movie as ineffable as light itself. You only need work with a mediocre cinematographer once to understand the contribution of the true talents in the field. They are technocrats, light painters, and your best on-set partners. The men and women who report directly to them—the gaffer, electrician, key grip and his team—

comprise the largest percentage of what's called "the shooting crew." In addition, on set are the make-up, hair, wardrobe, and effects teams, the assistant director and his/her staff, and endless specialists, but it is the director of photography ("DP") who is the director's key ally (or sadly, in some cases, enemy), determining the visualization of the material and the pace at which it is achieved.

Therefore, when I decide on the DP, it is a careful choice.

Many of my first candidates were busy, which is always the case. The length of any film's commitment for a cinematographer ranges from six months to a year. Statistically, the odds are not good for finding that your first choice DP is available exactly when needed. Inevitably, there are those people you might want to hire but who read the script and pass for one reason for another. They don't feel in sync with the material or the director or whatever.

Left: Director of photography Simon Duggan. **Above:** *Concept illustrations by The Aaron Sims Company of the three-headed dragon and a desiccated slave warrior who rises from the dead to fight the Emperor.*

The list quickly goes from ten primary names to "who have I not worked with but whose work I have admired?"

There was another consideration besides artistic achievement in this *Mummy* formula, as well. What I had in mind was huge, really huge. To achieve it in the time allowed by a large but, as usual, not quite large enough budget would require a DP who had speed as well as ease with the blend of on-set and 800 visual effects shots I had storyboarded. I needed someone with a relentless desire to suck every ounce of meat out of the lobster shell, and someone who'd demonstrated the ability to accomplish all of the above with artistry.

Now, the list got really short.

And on it was a name I knew, connected to a man I didn't: Simon Duggan.

I'd loved Alex Proyas's *I, Robot*, starring Will Smith and shot by Duggan. I'd been fascinated by Len Wiseman's *Underworld* movies, the second installment of which was also shot by him. These two movies proved Duggan could handle both a large-scale, big-budget and a low-budget effects film with great style.

I looked at Simon's extensive commercial reel and set up a Skype interview with him through his agent. Broadcast on my Macbook Pro screen was the image of a taciturn but charming man who had a real feeling for the challenges that my film would bring and a willingness to shoulder his end of the burden. There was a twinkle in his bright blue eyes, and wisdom in his Aussie/Kiwi-accented words.

I hired him on the spot.

"What, without meeting me?" he asked.

"I just met you," I replied. "We'll make your deal. Get on a plane."

Getting Down to Work

Nigel and I had less than six months to get the entire film conceptualized, designed, drawn, budgeted, and built, so our first two months were critical. Quickly, we exhausted several researchers. Sanja and Nigel put up massive boards with collages of photos of the art and architecture of the time, clothes, objects, maps, vehicles, and weapons. The walls of our offices were now covered in immersion wallpaper. Meanwhile, I was reading everything I could find on the terra-cotta army of Xi'an, the "Warring States" period before China's unification, the Great Wall, and the First Emperor's quest for immortality. Every day "Nigie," as I came to call him, and I would sit in my office and discuss the requirements of each set, the scale, and the needs called for by either the action in the script or those sequences I was still creating. Nigel proved to be an artist of the first magnitude; he thinks through the mechanical lead pencil he always carries. Sketches poured out of him and, with each one, some aspect of the movie became clearer and we could choose where to be literal with the periods and where to take license. Then he'd turn over his sketches to the production illustrators and, when they were done, we would discuss it further.

Production design not only gives a movie cohesion, it also influences the actors. When good actors walk on such a set, the very nature of the environment affects their performance. The place and the details speak to them, give them opportunities to use the space and to use the details as props. If you give Brendan Fraser a chance to use a prop, he'll run with it. Give him a good prop, he will run farther and faster. The set is a creative player in the orchestra of a scene. It influences everything that takes place within it. Sometimes it's a soloist, sometimes a harmonic line, but production design is a constant voice that plays richly to the audience through the eyes. If the film has the cohesion and richness we seek as viewers, it all begins here.

As close as I worked with Nigel and Sanja, there comes a time when you must let the talent you've attracted to the film be independent. I like to give guidelines and tonal goals and let each department head create in his/her own world without too much interference after this point. There is so much for a director to do at once that micromanaging, at least for me, seems overpossessive and counterproductive. Hire people you trust and then trust them.

Whenever they were ready to present, Nigel or Sanja would come down to my office and unveil their vision. Reviewing those presentations of art (some of which adorn

these pages) constituted some of the most thrilling moments in the entire production for me. I had wanted to make one of the most visually stunning action/adventure films ever seen and thanks to Nigel, Sanja, and their respective teams, my dream came true—one set and one costume at a time.

On July 23, 2007, we assembled in the "Rotunda" set meant to be the spare wing of the Shanghai museum. Brendan, Maria, and Luke were in formal evening wear, Isabella Leong wore her long, flowing Tibetan coat, Anthony Wong and Jessy Meng were dressed in their fascist warlord uniforms, and David Calder wore his three-piece suit, all original clothes created by Sanja Hays. The set designed by Nigel Phelps was expansive and architecturally rich, expertly dressed by Anne Kuljian. All sorts of archaeological tools and samples were scattered on various tables, just as they would be in the Smithsonian or a Cairo museum. Every detail was accurate. Simon and I had worked out a lighting/color scheme and the lamps were all in place; cutters, c-stands, gobos hung by the grips in tangles were scattered around the set. After a massive amount of time and effort, our movie was ready to take life.

This book showcases a small sampling of that enormous effort. To include everything would have required dozens of volumes, so we had to narrow our vision down to fit these pages. Here you'll find the core of our movie and get an inkling of the creative process that was our jumping-off place.

All movies share a creative process, but each one is unique in its own right. Ours began in an office above a coffee shop in Santa Monica, traveled innumerable miles around the globe, utilized the work of thousands of people, and then returned to southern Los Angeles for post-production.

Every film is also a journey in which you learn new things about life at every level. In the end, our time with the Mummy—like every other profound life experience—was far more amazing and enlightening than any of us ever anticipated. ■

Above: Brendan Fraser on the Foundation Chamber set.
Photo by Frank Masi.

The Making Of
The Mummy: Tomb of
the Dragon Emperor

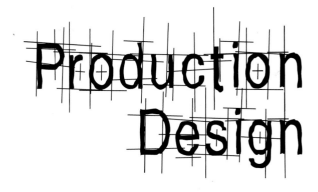

Production Design

€ven at his very first meeting with Rob Cohen, production designer Nigel Phelps knew he was embarking on an immensely challenging and creative journey. "This was a fantastic opportunity to create something that simply had never been seen before," explains Phelps. "These sort of design jobs don't come along that often and Rob gave me the chance to show off. The job also presented a whole series of complicated challenges enlisting the skill and talents of four separate art departments in three countries and on an accelerated schedule."

Working with Rob and producer Chris Brigham, the filmmakers' first task was to consider multiple available options regarding how and where to shoot the physical aspects of the film. Early on in pre-production, producer Sean Daniel introduced Phelps to Hengdian, an enormous back lot and studio facility located four hours south of Shanghai. "The sheer scale and enormity of this place was completely overwhelming," exclaims Phelps. "When you first skip through the website, you actually cannot believe your eyes; it's massive! It's an enormous back-lot that is always being used for Chinese films and TV. It's a remarkable complex of environments that cover many different periods in Chinese history and include several villages from different Chinese dynasties. They have even rebuilt the Forbidden City, the whole thing! Progress is happening so rapidly in China that a lot of the

Previous page: Jet Li standing before the dramatic Mausoleum to rally his terra-cotta warriors into battle. Left: Overview of the Stupa Courtyard set in Montreal, Canada.

old architecture is being rebuilt. They are recreating that architecture in Hengdian as a way of preserving it."

The other amazing thing about Hengdian was the fact that Phelps had never even heard of it. With many years of experience in the business, he thought he knew all the great studio facilities. "But discovering this place really hammered home how little we know about working in China," Phelps continues. "It got us thinking about how much other unique scenery we could discover there, too."

The creative production team in L.A. included several illustrators headed by Matt Codd, and a team of model makers led by Jamie Miller. John Dexter was the supervising art director who helped form the initial direction of how and where the film should be made. This was when set decorator Anne Kuljian joined the team.

After a couple of months in L.A., it was decided that Montreal would be the best place to design and build the bulk of the stage work. An art department headed by super-vising art director Isabelle Guay began to take shape in Canada, along with a conceptual team of local illustrators—Meinert Hanson, Henry Fong, Patrick Desgreniers, Christian de Massy, and Sean Samuels. The crew spent months figuring out the details of a whole series of very complicated sets. Mathieu Giguere and Ronny Gosselin were also instrumental in realizing a number of the sets in model form.

The benefits of working in Canada were apparent from the start. "You get a 'modern' art department in Montreal," says Phelps. "It's young and creative in its approach to designing and building the sets. The whole drafting team worked only on computers, and every set was pre-visualized in sketch-up model form. One of the striking things that occurred to me in Montreal was the economy of materials. When you walk around the back of a set, it usually consists of a forest of scaffolding and timber, especially with the sort of organic 'cave' type structures we were making for this film. But there was none of that in Montreal. It was all so clean and empty behind the sets that I would constantly point out to Michael Brochu, the head construction manager, how blown away I was at the economy of it all."

In contrast to the minimalist approach behind the sets, the degree of texture and detail applied to the surfaces on the other side was more than anyone in L.A. could imagine. A team of sculptors, headed by Rene Casavant, along with Ken Barley, the head plasterer, produced hundreds of beautiful figures and carvings to dress into

Above: Every piece of furniture was hand-painted and finished in great detail. Opposite: Elaborately hand-carved statues and the color gold were used repeatedly in designing the sets.

the sets. Alain Giguerre, the head scenic, completed the sets with some exceptionally fine finishes that amazed the crew. "I got so many constant remarks, not just from Rob, but the whole crew, about how impressed they were with the finishes all the time," says Phelps. "That does make you feel very proud to be working with such a talented group of people."

The Mummy Style

The basic style of the movie evolved from Rob Cohen's keen interest in and appreciation of Chinese culture. The director insisted that the basic look of the movie and every element of its design be grounded in actual Chinese art and architecture in order to bring a sense of realism into this action adventure. "Rob is Buddhist and he's very knowledgeable about Chinese culture," explains Phelps, "so it was important that we make everything as accurate and believable as possible. I really love the research process and learning about the culture, people, and places mentioned in the story. This script in particular had tons of fascinating examples. The range spread from ancient Chinese cities, temples, and palaces in 200 B.C., to a made-up culture in the far west of China, to the mysterious Himalayas, including Shangri-la, as well as the world of Shanghai in 1946."

Prompted by Cohen and pressured by a very tight deadline, Phelps began an intensive period of research that continued throughout the production. "From the very start

of the project, the film was a rush," he says. "As a result, the design process was very nonlinear and the sets were conjured up initially from the mind, and then as research started coming in and locations were found, we could start the layering process of the design. By adding all these elements you find in reality, it helps give the fantasy aspect of the scenery an added dimension. It was very important to Rob and I that you really believed these places could actually exist and not feel like a sound stage."

Color Me Gold

In determining the basic color theme of the movie, Nigel Phelps chose a variety of looks to complement the way the story flows. This was his jumping-off point. "When I first read the script, I tried to imagine the scenes in very broad terms," he explains. "That's when the shapes and tone of each environment are initially formed. Then I make a very detailed set list and weigh up how much action is taking place in each scene. All these factors help me determine the lighting and color pacing for the environments. Lighting is as integral to me as the choice of colors on the walls. It is, in fact, one of the same things, light and shadow working with color and form."

With DP Simon Duggan, Phelps discovered a kindred spirit. "We seemed to have similar taste and got along very well with one another," explains Phelps. "It's important to me to have a good relationship with the DP because in the design process I like to consider how the set will be lit, especially if it's on a stage and I have to build in particular lighting. I would have meetings, prior to any construction, with the DP and director to collaboratively discuss all set designs, and to determine from Simon what he needed, too.

"One of the first sets we created was the Stupa courtyard. Rob had suggested using 'thangas' to decorate the courtyard walls and Alain Giguerre, the painter, came up with the idea of using gold leaf on certain sections of the frescoes there. It worked so well that gold leaf became a binding element and thread for the whole film. I think we had some form of it in just about every set." ∎

Costumes

Costume designer Sanja Hays faced a huge challenge dressing the characters for the opening scenes of *The Mummy: Tomb of the Dragon Emperor*. Here, the action takes place in 200 B.C. China. In keeping with the idea of maintaining authenticity in all aspects of the film, Sanja had to ask herself: How did people dress back then?

"There was very little to go on," explains the designer. "There was some reference to jewelry that had been discovered from the period, a few drawings, a little bit of cloth, and some mummies that had been unearthed. I based most of my ideas on research I did from museums and books. The most useful were the findings from Xi'an where they found the terra-cotta warriors. We actually went there to look at them."

For Hays, the design process incorporates working both with the character and with the actor wearing the costume. "Part of my research was looking at the actors and their movies to see what they are about; how they move, how they behave," she says. "Then you think about the characters and what they are trying to project."

In the end, Hays married her artistic vision of the period with director Rob Cohen's vision for the scenes to create costumes that were based on the small amount of reference she'd been able to uncover. Almost all of the costumes had to be created from scratch because they didn't exist in any costume rental house.

"I had two very talented sketch artists working nonstop for about four months," says Hays. "They were

Hundreds of different outfits, uniforms, pieces of armor, and weapons were created. Illustrations by Christian Cordell and Phillip Boutte.

literally sitting next to me so I was able to make changes. After the sketches were approved, the second part of the creative process began—looking for fabrics. In the end, we got fabric from literally all over the world, including Hong Kong, mainland China, Thailand, India, Europe, New York, Europe, and Montreal. We used hundreds and hundreds of yards and a lot of silk, partly because of the Chinese theme but also because of the way it drapes and how beautifully it takes dye."

Hays was responsible for supervising a huge team in two continents. At an enormous workshop at Mel's Cité du Cinéma in Montreal she employed craftsmen from every area of expertise: a sketch artist, cutter-fitters, embroiderers, jewelry makers. All together, her team created thousands of costumes.

Jet Li

Designing the armor for Jet Li's character, the Emperor, was an enormous challenge for Sanja Hays. "It was the first thing I designed because everyone needed to know what the armor was going to be, in particular the visual effects and art departments," says Hays. "Initially I got into these philosophical discussions with Rob about the Emperor and his search for immortality. We realized that jade in ancient China was connected with immortality and

Above: Costume designer Sanja Hays with the final armor costume for the Emperor. Costume illustrations by Christian Cordella.

that he may have been dressed in jade just before he died. Rob and I got very excited because armor had never been made out of jade. Then the search started for the perfect piece of jade to give it the color, and how to make it. Each piece is individually done and they are connected."

Hays had to design several versions of the armor, as each of them had a different purpose. "For the scenes where he walks around and looks majestic, we created the heavier outfits, which used the replica jade pieces. We had to come up with a much lighter version for the fight sequences so he is able to move properly, and finally we needed a version for VFX when he turns into a terra-cotta warrior covered in mud and goo."

After much testing, the final action costume was held together with magnets.

Brendan Fraser

For Brendan Fraser, Hays wanted to create a look that was different from the first two movies. "I tried to give Brendan a more mellow, more kind of John Wayne look," she explains. "Unlike the previous two movies, here he wears a few suits. And because he is so built now, he looks terrific in the '40s-style menswear."

Of course, as Rick O'Connor, Fraser still needed action outfits. "We put him in a bomber jacket to kind of toughen him up as the action begins," says Hays, "and towards the end of the movie he goes back to his 'mummy chaser' look. Pants, shirts, and big guns, so he becomes the Rick O'Connell everyone knows."

Luke Ford

Designing for Luke Ford was a fun prospect for Hays. "Luke has a few different looks," explains Hays. "He starts the movie kind of down and dirty; a Marlboro man kind of thing with a 1946 leather jacket, unshaven. He carries that look really beautifully, as he is so tall and has

Opposite: Costume illustrations by Phillip Boutte for Rick O'Connell (left) and Alex O'Connell. Right: Costume illustrations by Christian Cordella for Lin.

such great charisma," says Hays. "Then we clean him up and switch him into the white tuxedo, Bogart style. Alex is more like a '40s hip-hop, with the big, baggy pilot pants, big old shoes, big jacket; it all is very proper period, but the silhouette is much more modern, and more appealing."

Isabella Leong

Isabella Leong's character, Lin, is first seen in the movie as an anonymous assassin. "In the Mausoleum she is guarding the Emperor's tomb," says Sanja Hays. "I wanted her tunic to keep her hidden because in the beginning

everyone thinks she is a man. She is like a kind of moving shadow."

For her next appearance, in the Shanghai Museum, Lin helps save Rick and Evy. "For this scene, I wanted her to be a little dressed up for Chinese New Year," says Hays, "so we put her in a coat, a little bit *Matrix* style. She needed to be ready for action, so we added dress pants underneath. The coat is cut long, so when she flies through the air it flies behind her."

Lin also needed an outdoor costume for her trek in the snow. "One of the most interesting costumes is the one which she wears when she goes to the Himalayas," explains Hays. "It's inspired by the Tibetan national costumes. I looked at a few books, and then did research at the UCLA library, where I discovered an amazing book of Tibetan costumes. So we decided to buy the book; we found one copy in Italy. I don't know what we ever did before the Internet!"

Michelle Yeoh

In this movie, Michelle Yeoh wears nine different costumes and each one of them is quite magnificent in its own right. "The fun part of designing for Michelle Yeoh's character, Zi Yuan, is that her costumes are not so determined by the period," Hays explains. "Zi Yuan is a sorceress who has been alive for more than 2,000 years, so I had a lot of freedom. My inspiration began with traditional Chinese clothes and blossomed from there."

Hays claims that part of the joy of designing for Yeoh was how well the actress moved in the clothes. "Michelle was not available for fittings, so we used another girl, but when Michelle finally put on the clothes, they came alive," says Hays. "She is so graceful; the way she holds her neck and moves, it's almost like she is floating. Michelle wears the clothes beautifully."

One of Yeoh's most important outfits was for a climactic swordfight with Jet Li, a scene that, incidentally, was the first ever to feature a fight between these two Asian superstars.

This particular outfit, which needed to be both stylish and functional, was inspired by Chinese ethnic minority clothes. While shopping in Shanghai, Hays bought a knee-length skirt for herself. "I swirled in it and was amazed by the way it moved," explains Hays. "We made a long version of the skirt, but it was not an easy task. One of the seamstresses, Malika, went through hell trying to figure out the construction on this hand-pleated garment. The skirt is very straight when Michelle is standing, but when she kicks, fights, and swirls, it flies out in a full circle." ■

Michelle Yeoh in the Shangri-la cave set. Four costume illustrations by Christian Cordella of the nine costumes produced and worn by Zi Yuan.

35

Special Effects

Creating the incredible action sequences in *The Mummy: Tomb of the Dragon Emperor* required a seamless blend of visual and mechanical effects. The visual effects department was helmed by VFX producer Ginger Theisen whose impressive track record includes a long run with ILM. With over 800 VFX shots to complete, Theisen brought on two digital houses: Digital Domain, headed by VFX supervisors Matt Butler and Joel Hynek, and Rhythm and Hues, headed by VFX producer Derek Spears.

"There is an amazing range of effects in this movie," explains Derek Spears, "including everything from awe-inspiring characters to big effects shots like avalanches. We've got huge battle sequences with massive numbers of digital characters: a complete gambit for everything from practical effects to computer-generated characters to computer digital environments."

The SFX department boasted SFX supervisor Bruce Steinheimer whose credits include *Gangs of New York, Mission Impossible 2, Face/Off*, and many others. In order to create the large number of mechanical effects employed in the movie, Steinheimer had to oversee four different VFX

shops in both Montreal and China. "It was a big logistical challenge for me," admits Steinheimer. "We had over 100 people working in effects on different continents at the same time in order to make sure all the effects would be ready for both the main and the action units." ◼

Above: A previsualization illustration of the terra-cotta Emperor by the Aaron Sims Company. Below left: Stunt coordinator Mark Southworth, SFX supervisor Bruce Steinheimer, mechanical effects supervisor Joe Viskocil, Rob Cohen, and VFX supervisor Derek Spears. Below: Animation supervisor Craig Talmy (from Rhythm and Hues), VFX producer Ginger Theisen, and unit publicist Amanda Brand.

Locations

The Mummy: *Tomb of the Dragon Emperor* was filmed over a five-month period on two continents: Montreal, Canada, and Beijing and Shanghai in China.

Principal photography kicked off on July 26, 2007, at Mel's Cité du Cinéma in Montreal with a powerful action sequence set in the Shanghai Museum and then moved on to the Stupa courtyard set. Another set portrayed the mountains of the Himalayas and the hidden Gateway to Shangri-la. These sets were covered with fake snow and one night a huge storm hit the set, washing away all the snow. The set dressing team was called in the early hours to repair the damage, and when the crew arrived at 7:00 A.M. there was no sign of any damage.

The production then moved out to the ADF stage about 40 minutes from Mel's Cité du Cinéma. There, production designer Nigel Phelps created the awe-inspiring Mausoleum, which is filled with thousands of terra-cotta warriors and a series of deadly booby traps.

Returning to Mel's Cité du Cinéma, the cast and crew moved into the mysterious world of the Foundation Chamber, the setting for the brutal hand-to-hand battle between the Emperor and Rick O'Connell. There was a tremendous buzz of excitement on the set, as this was the first scene shot with superstar Jet Li.

Following the brutal fight and the incredible action sequence, the production moved into the tranquillity of the Shangri-la cave which shimmered with candlelight, illuminating a gigantic and magnificent sleeping Buddha

Rob Cohen on the massive Shangri-la set at Mel's Cité du Cinéma in Montreal, Canada.

that lay along the length of it. The alcoves were filled with beautiful carved statues, and a stunning pagoda stood at the entry.

Filming in Montreal was a great experience for all involved, as the city boasts some of the most talented technicians in the world. After 54 days, filming in Canada was completed and the production company prepared for their next great adventure: shooting in China!

The China Experience

The Canadian shoot ended on October 11, 2007, and, amazingly, work resumed in China on October 16. That meant that the production had only four days to transport cast, crew, and equipment thousands of miles, halfway across the world in fact. One might have anticipated an enormous problem, but that is not what happened. "The move from Montreal to China was smooth," marvels Rob Cohen. "Our executive producer Chris Brigham, Chinese producers Chiu Wah Lee and Doris Tse Kasr Wai, and the China production supervisors Mitch Dauterive and Er Dong Liu actually performed a miracle. To move 200 westerners on a Friday to shoot on Tuesday seemed virtually impossible, but they did it!"

Of course, work in China started long before the cast and crew arrived on set. As early as February 2007, the

filmmakers were popping back and forth to Asia, looking for locations and gathering the all-important Chinese team which was headed by two main art directors, Yi Zhen Zhou and Olympic Lau. "Most Chinese art directors appear to be specialized," explains Nigel Phelps. "For example, Mr. Yi, who is the art director for the 200 B.C. scenes, specializes in that period. Olympic, on the other hand, specializes in the 1940s and art-directed all the Shanghai streets and the Imhoteps nightclub. One of the remarkable things about this film is that absolutely everything had to be designed and built. They don't have the same sort of prop houses in China as we do in L.A., so you can't rent hardly anything. Every sign, lamppost, and vehicle had to be created; it was a huge undertaking."

Once in China, the head count of the cast and crew grew enormously. At one point, there were over 2,000 people on the payroll. The multicultural crew was comprised of 200 Americans and Quebecoise, 1,700 from mainland China, 100 from Hong Kong, and a few other Malaysians, Croatians, Slovenians, and Taiwanese.

For the Chinese shoot, work initially began in Tianmo, a desert area located in Inner Mongolia, about two hours north of Beijing. "The Tianmo location was chosen because it was possible to build five major sets within five minutes of each other and all with different-looking backgrounds," says Nigel Phelps.

On his daily blog, Rob Cohen wrote about arriving on set that first morning in China: "The dawn is breaking over the Great Wall, the original wall made of tamped earth that towers over the horizon. The sun is real: I had the wall built. Hundreds of our Chinese art department labored for months to prepare the site. The Dragon Emperor himself

*Left: The shoot in Tianmo, China, began with a traditional "good luck" ceremony. From left to right: Chiu Wah Lee (line producer, China), Brendan Fraser, Rob Cohen, Vic Armstrong (action unit director), Chris Brigham (executive producer), and Sean Daniel (producer). **Opposite:** The Great Wall.*

will mount a 50-foot-high colossus to wake his 5,000 Terra-cotta Warriors from 20 centuries underground and lead them in one final battle against the O'Connells and the mystical forces of his ancient enemy, Ming Guo. Armies will clash. Good versus Evil. The Living against the Undead. In other words, it's Monday on the set of *The Mummy: Tomb of the Dragon Emperor.*"

The Tianmo location was the setting for several scenes, including the epic battle sequence at the climax of the movie and the incredible sword fight between Jet Li and Michelle Yeoh.

"In order to create the battlefield it was necessary to design something that was graphically recognizable so that you would instantly know which side the terra-cotta army was coming from and which were the foundation warriors," explains Nigel Phelps. "Basically it was just a big empty space. I created the ruins to add interest. They were supposed to be the vestiges of a palace, and they looked very believable."

Other scenes shot in Tianmo were of Yang's camp, which was constructed in a Ming Dynasty village located in a complex of caves close to the Tianmo location, and the interior of the black tent where the Emperor meets with his generals.

During the shoot in Tianmo, the crew was housed in Yanqing, about an hour's drive from the set. Yanqing is known as a summer resort city for Beijing residents and is very close to the Badaling section of the Great Wall. The roads in the area were heavily congested with trucks transporting goods in and out of the city. Consequently, the production and transportation teams devised an amazing support system by stationing staff along the entire way to direct the movie vehicles along the best route for the time of day. The system worked smoothly for the majority of the time, saving hours of traffic congestion for the cast and crew at the end of a long day.

The production was extremely fortunate with the weather in China, although there was one day when a

sandstorm hit the area. Filming continued, but it made life difficult for the whole crew, especially the camera crew and the actors.

Toward the end of the shoot, temperatures dropped rapidly and the production gratefully retreated south to Shanghai. Shooting then continued at the Shanghai Film Studios, about an hour's drive outside the city.

The studio boasted an enormous set devoted to the streets of Shanghai in the 1900s—one reason the production decided to come to Shanghai. This was the setting for the chariot chase through the streets of 1946 Shanghai on the eve of the Chinese New Year.

The Shanghai studio also housed several other sets including the Emperor's Throne room, a magnificent testament to Chinese craftsmanship.

The final scenes of the shoot took place in Imhoteps,

a marvelous 1940s Egyptian-style nightclub. "Imhoteps was a very important set both because it has a huge page count and because it had been engineered by Rob to be the last set we shot on, so we could have our wrap party there," laughs Nigel Phelps. "I tried to make it feel as if this is Rob's nod to the other movies, but I wanted it to be a believable place that you'd expect to find in Shanghai at that time; kind of glamorous and larger than life."

While the main unit finished their work at the studio, the action unit moved on to shoot a dramatic battle sequence at Hengdian World Studios, four hours drive

The construction of the Great Wall of China was the concept for the opening scene in the movie. The idea was that the Emperor's conquered enemies were buried in the foundation and would, in the climactic final battle, rise up to seek their vengeance against him.

south of Shanghai. One of the largest studios in Asia, it boasts life-size replicas of the Emperor Qin's palace, Qing Ming Shang He Tu, the Palaces of the Ming and Quing Dynasties, and the Grand Hall of Dazhi Temple with a figure of Sakyamuni 28.8 meters high, the tallest indoor figure of Buddha in China.

That's a Wrap!

After 91 days of shooting and 2,021 shots, *The Mummy: Tomb of the Dragon Emperor* finally wrapped in the early morning hours of November 30, 2007.

At a press conference just prior to the completion of filming in Shanghai, Rob Cohen announced, to great excitement, that the movie's premiere would take place in Beijing on July 26, 2008, just before the start of the Beijing Olympics.

"China is on the front page of the newspapers almost every day now," says Cohen. "It was a great place to set a movie that has fantasy, imagery, history, and incredible action. I would like people to feel that the culture of China has been dealt with fairly and beautifully."

To celebrate the wrap of principal photography in truly Chinese style, SFX supervisor Bruce Steinheimer created a mind-blowing fireworks display that lasted nearly eight minutes. Crew members, who inevitably become blasé to the excitement of explosions, stunts, and other daily events, stood wide-eyed and open-mouthed at the incredible showstopper. There couldn't have been a more fitting end to the roller-coaster action adventure that gave birth to *The Mummy: Tomb of the Dragon Emperor.* ∎

The Cast

Brendan Fraser RICK O'CONNELL

Jet Li THE EMPEROR

Maria Bello EVELYN O'CONNELL

Luke Ford ALEX O'CONNELL

John Hannah JONATHAN CARNAHAN

Isabella Leong LIN

Russell Wong MING GUO

Michelle Yeoh ZI YUAN

Part One

The Ancient World

China, 200 B.C.

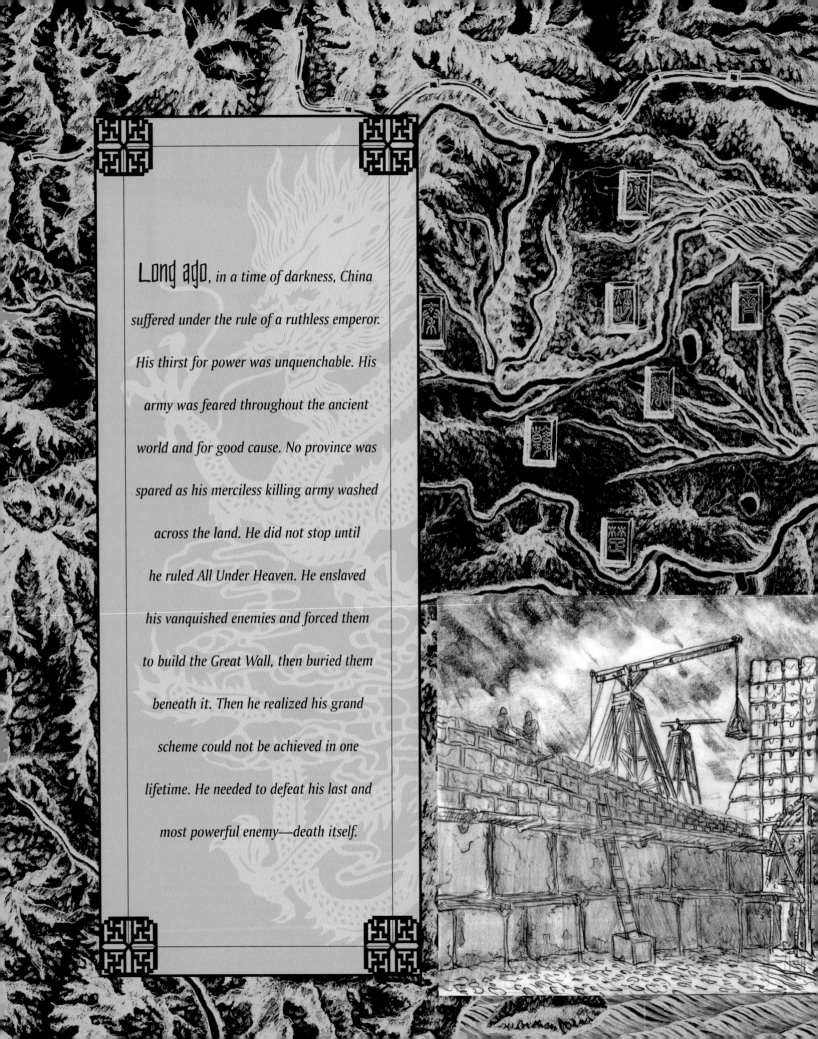

Long ago, *in a time of darkness, China suffered under the rule of a ruthless emperor. His thirst for power was unquenchable. His army was feared throughout the ancient world and for good cause. No province was spared as his merciless killing army washed across the land. He did not stop until he ruled All Under Heaven. He enslaved his vanquished enemies and forced them to build the Great Wall, then buried them beneath it. Then he realized his grand scheme could not be achieved in one lifetime. He needed to defeat his last and most powerful enemy—death itself.*

Building the Great Wall

Concept drawings by Ricardo Delgado showing how the Great Wall was built.

The opening scene in the movie reveals a panoramic view of China's Great Wall, one of the most extraordinary feats of construction in human

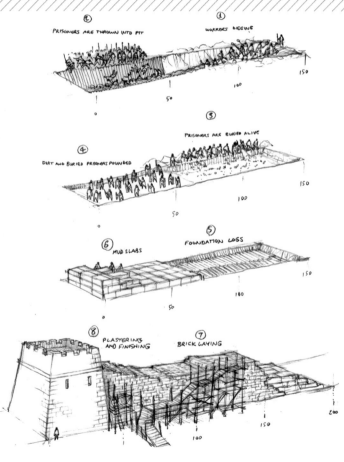

① PRISONERS ARE THROWN INTO PIT
② WORKERS DIGGING

③ PRISONERS ARE BURIED ALIVE
④ DIRT AND BURIED PRISONERS POUNDED

⑤ FOUNDATION LOGS
⑥ MUD SLABS

⑦ BRICK LAYING
⑧ PLASTERING AND FINISHING

history. This initial shot was meant to show that the Wall was, in essence, a mass grave for the victims of the Emperor's ruthless army. To convey this idea, the set was designed to be filmed as a backward track, showing how the Wall was constructed, before the camera turns around to reveal the sheer enormity of the task.

"Even though this scene in the film is really brief, it still is one of my favorite sets," says Nigel Phelps. "And it was shot on the actual site where the Wall was really built over 2100 years ago!"

Indeed, this amazing set was built in the desert area of Tianmo, about two hours northwest of Beijing, and adjacent to ruins of one of the iterations of the Wall itself. The set establishes all the extraordinary sets yet to be seen in the movie.

Left: Concept drawings of the 8 stages of the Great Wall construction by Meinert Hansen. Above, below, and opposite: Concept illustrations by Yi Zhen Zhou.

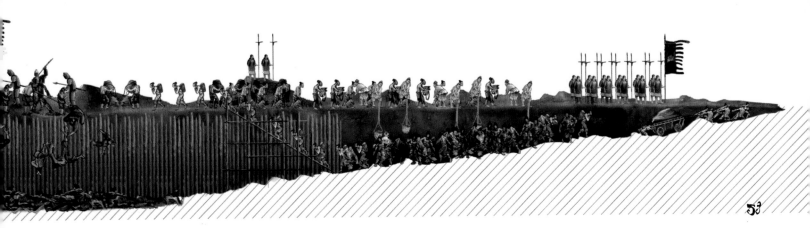

Opposite: Scale models of the Great Wall set. Opposite below: Concept drawing by Christian Robert de Massy. Left: Preliminary sketch by Meinert Hansen. Below: The Great Wall set under construction. Photos by Nigel Phelps.

The Pyramids of China

The pyramids shown at the beginning of the film are a great example of how fantasy blended with reality in the making of this film. "When we first came to China to scout in February 2007, we traveled to outer Mongolia to look at these sand dunes which turned out to be the size of Denmark," says production designer Nigel Phelps. "I was flipping through a brochure in the hotel where we were staying and I discovered these pyramids, so we raced off to see them. They were absolutely phenomenal. The landscape is very geographically similar to what we had in Tainmo—the foothills, the mountains and everything surrounding it. I thought Rob would love it, so I brought him the idea and he decided to use them for a scene at the beginning of the film. People will probably look at these pyramids and think they are CG because you just don't expect to see such things in China."

These four massive pyramids were actually in a valley of approximately 250 tombs. They contained the remains of a race of Chinese who were annihilated by the Mongolians because they shot the arrow that killed Genghis Khan. It was only a couple of hundred years ago that this completely forgotten land was un-covered. Archaeologists determined that these tombs are the only remaining vestiges of an entire culture.

PATRICK DESGRENIERS

These ancient pyramids in Mongolia were used as the background for the Emperor's Black Tent Camp. *Opposite: Photo of the site by Nigel Phelps. Above: Concept drawings by Patrick Desgreniers of the tents set amid the fantastic pyramids. Right: Storyboard panel of the scene by Meinert Hansen.*

Above and below: Storyboard panels by Meinert Hansen of the Black Tent Camp set. Left: Concept illustration of the Emperor's tent by Patrick Desgreniers.

The Black Tent Camp

The pyramids, the inspirational start of the Black Tent Camp sequence, now appear as the backdrop to this location.

The camp, in the foreground, was another rich exercise in detail for set decorator Anne Kuljian, whose job was to create different areas of interest for the camera to roam about and discover. Kuljian built a couple of kitchens, an armory, and a stable area; everything was beautifully detailed and felt completely real.

"When I was creating the Emperor's camp and the black tent, I was trying to design something that felt pretty unique, that felt appropriate for the Emperor's character," explains Nigel Phelps. "I found a book that showed some ancient Chinese reed houses. They were simple but very interesting shapes, and they became the basis for the tent designs. Patrick Desgreniers did some really nice drawings that picked up on this initial theme and turned them into something much more dark and ominous."

*Left: Scale model of the Emperor's tent. **Above:** A sketch of a cooking prop and the finished prop as it appeared on-screen. **Below:** The final working Black Tent exterior set.*

Below and right: Concept illustrations by Patrick Desgreniers of the interior of the Emperor's tent. *Above:* Rob Cohen examines the scale model of the Great Wall construction prop. *Opposite:* Floor plan of the interior of the tent.

Dressing a Tent

The interior of the tent had to be built separately to the exterior as a weather-covered set in the construction workshop, ten minutes away from set. Absolutely everything in the set was custom-designed and -built. All the light fixtures and metalwork were real bronze. "When I asked any of the Chinese crew why we weren't just making them from resin and painting them, they would always answer that it was quicker, cheaper, and better," marvels Phelps. "You can't beat the real thing!"

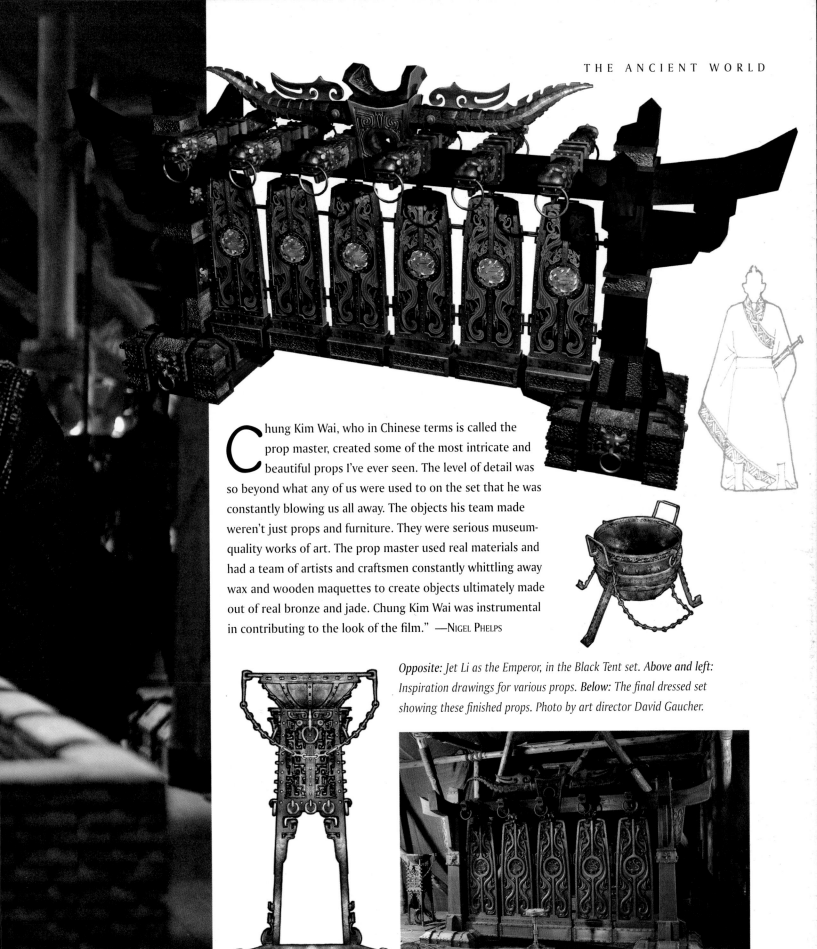

Chung Kim Wai, who in Chinese terms is called the prop master, created some of the most intricate and beautiful props I've ever seen. The level of detail was so beyond what any of us were used to on the set that he was constantly blowing us all away. The objects his team made weren't just props and furniture. They were serious museum-quality works of art. The prop master used real materials and had a team of artists and craftsmen constantly whittling away wax and wooden maquettes to create objects ultimately made out of real bronze and jade. Chung Kim Wai was instrumental in contributing to the look of the film." —NIGEL PHELPS

Opposite: Jet Li as the Emperor, in the Black Tent set. Above and left: Inspiration drawings for various props. Below: The final dressed set showing these finished props. Photo by art director David Gaucher.

The Palace

The design and geographical layout of the Emperor's palace, a key location at the start of the movie, had to be created. Production designer Nigel Phelps was inspired by an aerial photograph of the layout of the Temple of Heaven in Beijing. "I knew it was a perfect place for me to start," says Phelps. "It reminded me of geometric crop circles or something you'd see on the plains of Nazca. It made total sense to me in terms of the relationship between the palace and the mausoleum. Those were the two environments that needed to talk to each other and after seeing the layout of this traditional Chinese setting, everything fell into place."

Another challenge for this huge location was to find a basic color palette to unify the various elements of the set. "The original paint scheme of the palace in Hengdian was yellow and red," explains Phelps. "I wanted to make it feel much tougher and more as if they were accustomed to being at war and being attacked all the time, which was an important story point. So I added some old wood to create a more aggressive, 'fortified' look. It gave it a

much rougher quality. We also added a very dark wash over all of the paintwork so you were only really aware of brown and black."

Above: Inspirational concept drawing of the palace throne room entrance. Left: The throne room entrance by Patrick Desgreniers. Right: The final set.

65

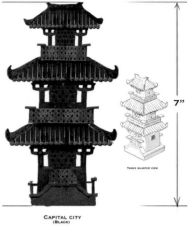

CAPITAL CITY
(BLACK)

7"

SECONDARY CITY
(TERRACOTTA)

SOLDIER
(BLACK)

Left and above: Concept
illustrations by Christian Robert
de Massy of the Emperor's
massive throne-room war map
and the map's movable pieces.
Below: Early concept drawing
by Patrick Desgreniers.

The Throne Room

The Throne Room was originally conceived as a huge imposing set overlooking the main Palace Courtyard, but as the script developed, the director and the production designer decided on a different approach that was better suited to the Emperor's character.

"The Emperor seemed more warlord than regal," explains Nigel Phelps. "He was a tough, hands-on warrior, much better suited to a heavily fortified elevated position up in the eaves of the palace roof with all of his most valuable possessions.

This position also gave him a better overview of the palace grounds."

The architectural style of the interior of the Throne Room was based on actual research but increased in scale to represent a more primitive forerunner to the traditional style of Chinese architecture. Windows and moldings were also exaggerated in scale to add emphasis to the power of the place.

The throne itself was

Above and below: Early concept drawings of the throne room by Christian Robert de Massy. Right: The final set.

carved out of solid wood, as was the huge 20' x 20' map table. "There was so much detail in there; it was a feast for the eyes," says Phelps.

We shot all the scenes in the Throne Room with a team of Chinese cultural advisors constantly helping me with the Qin dynasty language, ceremonies, and behaviors. We discovered that the 'art' and 'intellect' people would stand at the Emperor's left and 'military' at his right, musicians were not allowed to carry swords, no one ever turned their back to the Emperor, and on and on. But the film gods dwell in the details; even if it's a world that you are not familiar with, it feels true. Generalize them at your peril!" —ROB COHEN

Above: Costume illustration by Phillip Boutte.

Zi Yuan's Apothecary

Opposite: Michelle Yeoh (Zi Yuan) in her intricately designed Apothecary. Above: Illustration by Patrick Desgreniers. Below: The actual temple near Beijing, used as an exterior shot.

Near Beijing, we found this small temple on a bridge, perched in between this really narrow gorge. The only access was by way of a terrifically steep staircase cut into the rock. This location was an ideal setting for the secret apothecary Zi Yuan inherits after her father passes away.

"This scene was set in 200 B.C. so we needed the interior set to feature a ton of character. Architecturally, I wanted this very small, cramped space but with these huge ancient wooden beams that would make sense since it was lodged between two cliff walls, like in the exterior.

"The floor was sculpted as it was placed directly onto an existing stone floor.

"The dressing was thick with many weird and wonderful components from which to make spells and potions.

"Anne and her team did a beautiful job conveying a sense of logic and reality to a very fantastic and atmospheric set."

—Nigel Phelps

The Turfan Monastery

The concept of this set was to create a 200 BC Chinese equivalent to the ancient library at Alexandria. To this end, Nigel Phelps and his Chinese art directors looked at some interesting locations in the far west, toward the borders of Afghanistan, Kazakhstan, and Russia. The most interesting location was Turfan. "I'd never heard of Turfan until then," says Phelps, "but here was the crossroads of the world in terms of mixed cultures. Because of its Muslim and Chinese influences, the architectural style is very unique. I had originally thought of containing the library inside a Babel-like tower, with a path that wound its way up to a fortified entrance on the top, but after seeing these real structures in Turfan I decided to abandon that approach.

"Christian de Massy did some wonderfully evocative sketches of the exterior, which tried to combine two different locations, but the interior was another challenge altogether. We began researching what books looked like in that period, and quickly realized this period actually pre-dated 'books' as we know them. So the library became an eclectic collection of carvings into bones, slates, and stone tablets, and the Chinese method of creating scrolls made up of individually split bamboo.

"There were many great details that went into the making of the library, but one that really helps sell the ancient multicultural aspect of the set was to paint 'A–Z' on the shelves in eight different forgotten languages.

"The analogy of a compass isn't lost here either," adds Phelps, "with ancient versions of north, south, east, and west above the window, along with the four bridges to the central platform to emphasize the crossroads aspects of the set."

Top: Concept drawing by Syd Dutton from Illusion Arts, of the Turfan Monastery exterior. Above: Location shot of the actual site in Turfan that was the inspiration for the set by Nigel Phelps. Below: Michelle Yeoh (Zi Yuan) and Russell Wong (Ming Guo) searching the ancient texts.

Above: Concept drawing by Christian Robert de Massy of the interior of the ancient library.
Right: Ming Guo and Zi Yuan retrieve the Oracle Bones. Left and below: Concept illustrations of the key and the five steps that uncover Oracle Bones.

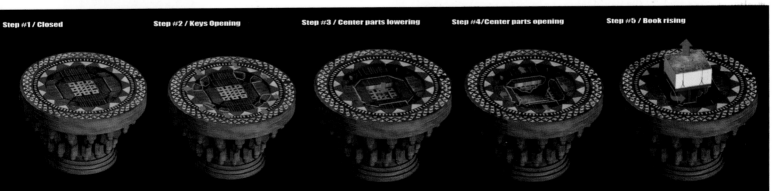

Step #1 / Closed   Step #2 / Keys Opening   Step #3 / Center parts lowering   Step #4/Center parts opening   Step #5 / Book rising

Left: Concept drawing of the Turfan bedroom by Christian Robert de Massy. *Above:* Concept illustration by Christian Robert de Massy of the bedroom door and the peephole that Li Zhou uses to spy on Zi Yuan and Ming Guo. *Below:* Final bedroom set; photograph by Nigel Phelps.

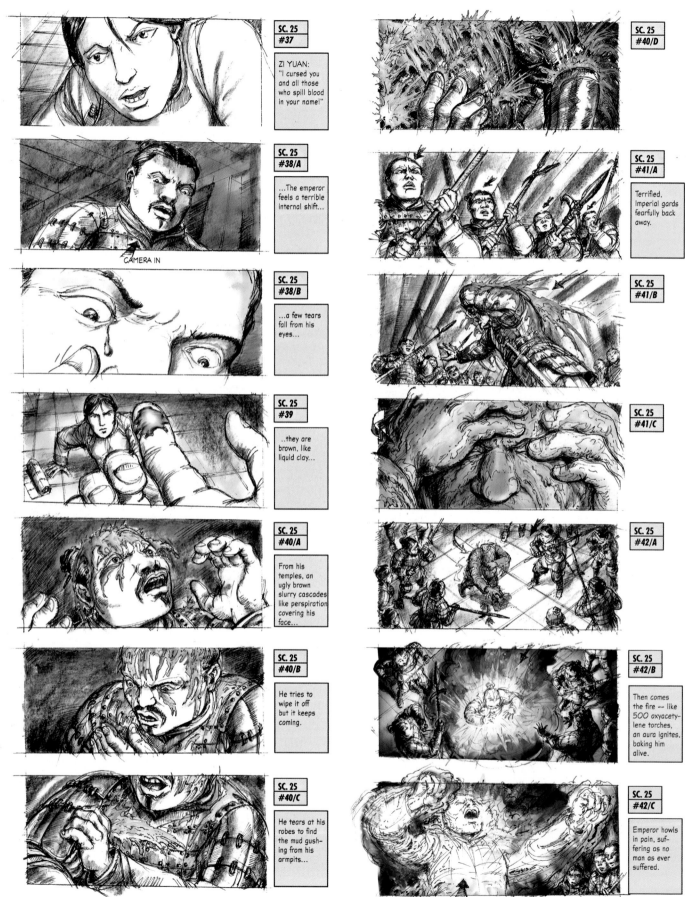

SC. 25
#37

ZI YUAN:
"I cursed you
and all those
who spill blood
in your name!"

SC. 25
#38/A

...The emperor
feels a terrible
internal shift...

CAMERA IN

SC. 25
#38/B

...a few tears
fall from his
eyes...

SC. 25
#39

..they are
brown, like
liquid clay...

SC. 25
#40/A

From his
temples, an
ugly brown
slurry cascades
like perspiration
covering his
face...

SC. 25
#40/B

He tries to
wipe it off
but it keeps
coming.

SC. 25
#40/C

He tears at his
robes to find
the mud gush-
ing from his
armpits...

SC. 25
#40/D

SC. 25
#41/A

Terrified,
Imperial gards
fearfully back
away.

SC. 25
#41/B

SC. 25
#41/C

SC. 25
#42/A

SC. 25
#42/B

Then comes
the fire -- like
500 oxyacety-
lene torches,
an aura ignites,
baking him
alive.

SC. 25
#42/C

Emperor howls
in pain, suf-
fering as no
man as ever
suffered.

The Terra-cotta Curse

Above and right: Photos of Jet Li turning into terra-cotta. Opposite and below: Storyboard panels by Francis Back of this scene.

CAMERA IN

Above: Michelle Yeoh puts a curse on Jet Li and then escapes. A great deal of work went into the design of the terra-cotta warriors, especially the statue of Jet Li. *Left:* Early concept of the Emperor's head. *Right:* 3-D rendering of a terra-cotta warrior. *Opposite:* The final illustration for the terra-cotta Emperor. Illustrations by the Aaron Sims Company.

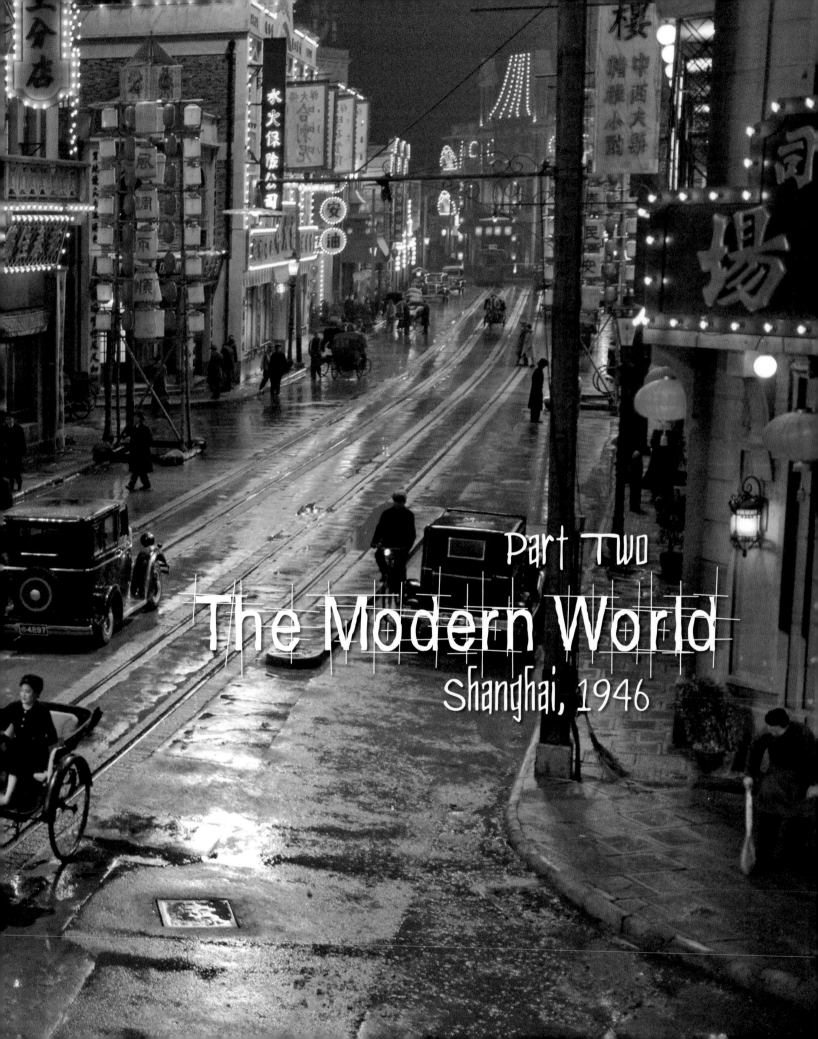

Part Two
The Modern World
Shanghai, 1946

*Opposite: Brendan Fraser (Rick) takes up a new hobby. **Above:** Location shots of the English mansion where the retired O'Connells live. **Left:** Concept drawing by Christian Robert de Massy of Rick's closet, indicating all the hobbies he's abandoned. **Below:** The O'Connell coat of arms by de Massy.*

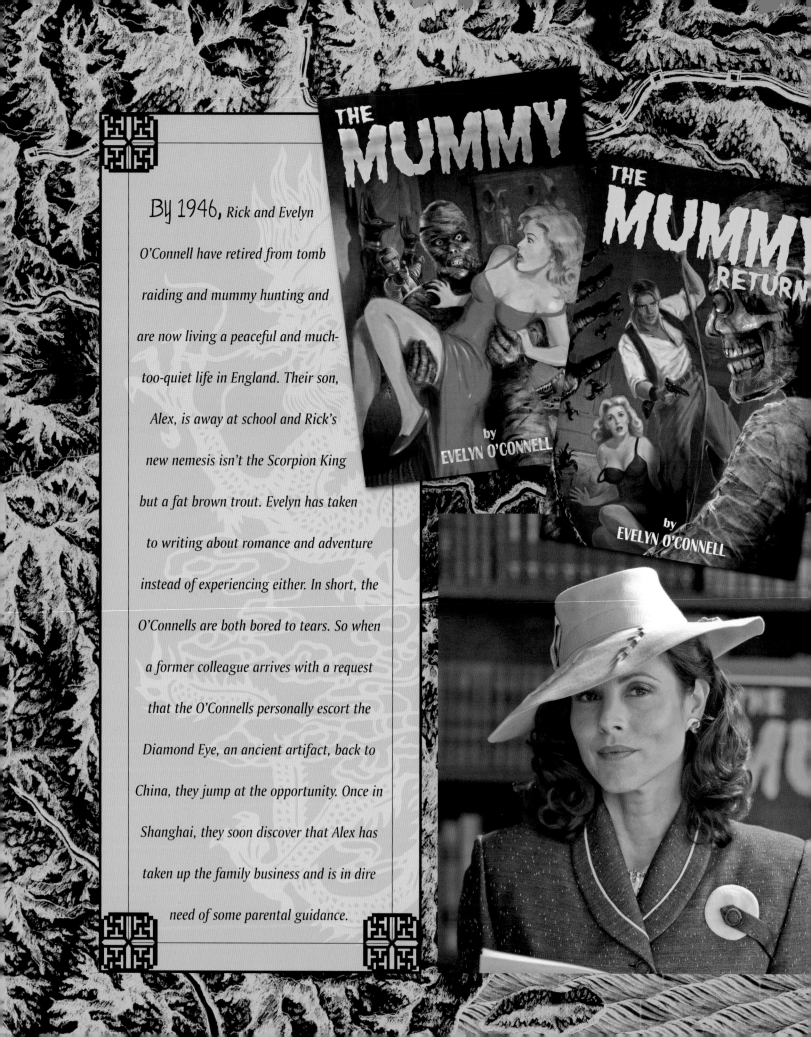

BY 1946, *Rick and Evelyn O'Connell have retired from tomb raiding and mummy hunting and are now living a peaceful and much-too-quiet life in England. Their son, Alex, is away at school and Rick's new nemesis isn't the Scorpion King but a fat brown trout. Evelyn has taken to writing about romance and adventure instead of experiencing either. In short, the O'Connells are both bored to tears. So when a former colleague arrives with a request that the O'Connells personally escort the Diamond Eye, an ancient artifact, back to China, they jump at the opportunity. Once in Shanghai, they soon discover that Alex has taken up the family business and is in dire need of some parental guidance.*

Left: In London, Maria Bello (Evelyn), having "retired" from chasing mummies, is now a successful author of romantic novels. Evelyn's book covers by Meinert Hansen. Above: *Rough sketch of the bookstore interior by Meinert Hansen. Right: Sketch of the bookstore exterior by Nigel Phelps. Below: The bookstore exterior set in Montreal, Canada.*

The Diamond Eye of Shangri-la

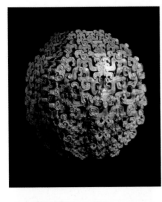 

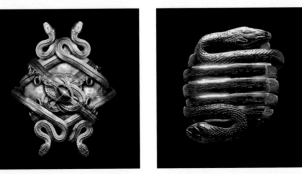

The O'Connells are asked to return the Diamond Eye to China, its rightful home. Legend has it that the Eye will point the way to the Pool of Eternal Life. The actual prop went through many incarnations. Drawings by Matt Codd. *Left:* Concept ilustration by Patrick Desgreniers. *Opposite:* The final Diamond Eye prop.

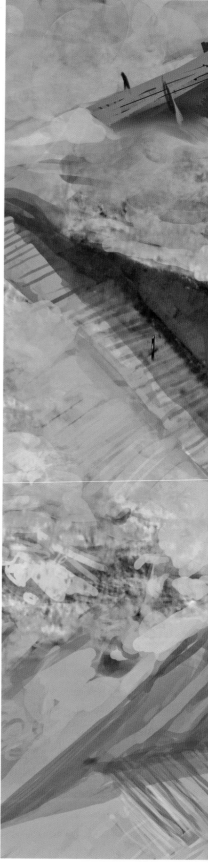

Ninghxia Excavation Site

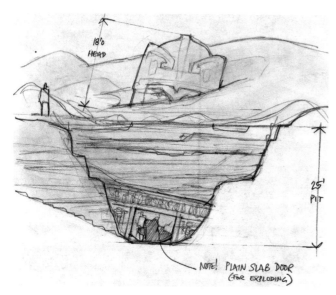

18'0 HEAD

25' PIT

NOTE! PLAIN SLAB DOOR (FOR EXPLODING)

Top: Concept drawing of the mausoleum by Ryan Church.
Above: Sketch by Nigel Phelps. Right: Illustration of the
excavation site by Patrick Desgreniers.

The excavation site, which is also the exterior of the mausoleum where the Emperor is entombed, was a gigantic set to design and build. Though this kind of architecture would not exist in China, the structure was important for a pivotal story point. Here, the Emperor addresses his army and Rob Cohen wanted to see Jet Li on a dramatic platform. "In the original design I had the Emperor's statue as a standing full figure surrounded by obelisks," explains Nigel Phelps. "When I showed Rob, he loved the

direction, but filmatically thought it worked better to shrink the figure down to just the head and shoulders. He had a very distinct image in his mind of Jet standing in the foreground with this massive head behind him. The only way to achieve that was to chop the body off so you were just left with a bust."

To create this image for the director, Phelps did extensive research on excavation sites in China. "We found some amazing-looking ones in China," says the production designer. "We were exceptionally lucky with the location that we picked in Tian Mo. The makeup of the soil enabled us to build what looks like an inverted pyramid, 30 feet deep. I was expecting we'd have to make the walls of the pit out of structural timber and scenically make it look like dirt. So I was really excited when the surveyor told us we could dig it for real.

"We also had the ability at this location to shoot both the 'discovery' pit and the 'excavated' pit almost side by side, so they would have the same light and distant background. I added a strategically placed sand dune in between, so you could shoot on both sets without seeing the other."

In the final film, there are three different versions of this set. The 200 B.C. version is a completely CG design. Then there is the 1946 half-uncovered version and, finally, the one that is shown in all its excavated glory, when it is completely exposed and makes for a dramatic backdrop for the final battle at the end of the film.

Right and below: Concept drawings of the mausoleum by Ryan Church. Bottom: Composite illustrations of the excavation site pre- and post-detonation.

Above and left: Scale models and concept drawing of the excavation site. This huge area was created in the desert of Inner Mongolia, and the filmmakers were delighted when told they could actually dig in the sand. Up until then, they had anticipated having to create backdrops to look like sand.

The Mausoleum

The incredible interior of the mausoleum was inspired by the ground layout of the Temple of Heaven in China and the Adalaj step well in India. "I found some pictures of this Indian step well; it was such a unique structure," says Nigel Phelps. "I'd never seen anything like it and it completely coincided with finding an aerial picture of this Chinese mausoleum. There is this enormous set of stairs which open to the sunlight and seem to go on forever. You go down the stairs deeper and deeper, then at the bottom, a hundred feet down, is a well with the water. It was so beautiful; the light was so gorgeous, as was the geometry of it. I loved

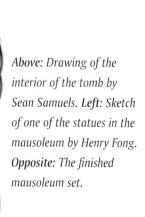

Above: Drawing of the interior of the tomb by Sean Samuels. Left: Sketch of one of the statues in the mausoleum by Henry Fong. Opposite: The finished mausoleum set.

it, so did Rob. Then it was a case of rationalizing that into something that looked Chinese and worked geographically for the scene. It just felt so natural; you get to the bottom of the stairs and instead of seeing a well, there is an even bigger space with thousands of terra-cotta warriors to lead you to the actual tomb entrance in the floor.

"Further into the set is another interesting element: the water compass, which was very ancient Chinese, so all those components really fell together nicely.

"Our 200 B.C. art director Mr. Yi brought so many fascinating details into the design, things none of us would know. Like the fact that when ancient Chinese armies attacked they'd bang on these gigantic drums and when retreating, they would sound these enormous bells. Mr. Yi suggested these as essential bits of set dressing to go in the Mausoleum. His involvement enabled me to go to a whole other level of detail with the sets."

Above left: Prop detail by Meinert Hansen. Above: Concept drawing of one of the killing devices inside the mausoleum by Henry Fong. Below: On-set photo of Albert Kwan (Chu Wah), Luke Ford (Alex O'Connell), and David Calder (Roger Wilson) finally gaining entrance into the tomb.

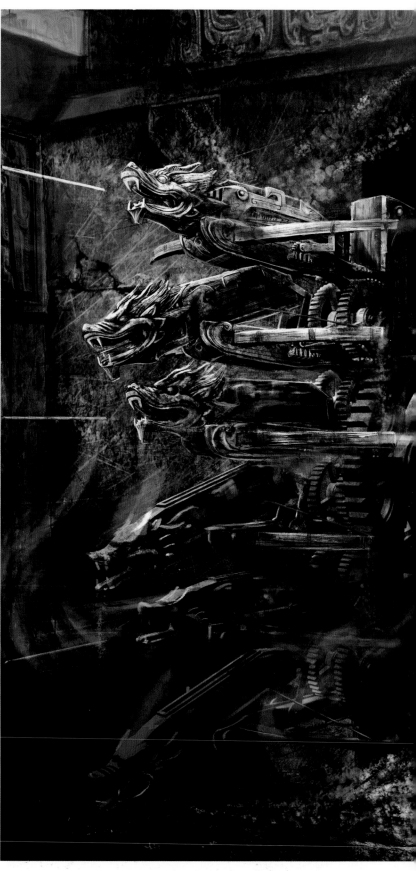

Working on this film, I discovered that technology was advanced in China at that time. The seismograph seen in the Mausoleum wasn't in the original script, but Rob added it when we discovered that the Chinese were using them more than five hundred years ago. They were used to warn them which direction an invading army would be approaching from, so it was a natural thing to incorporate into the mausoleum as an early warning system to trigger the automated crossbow defenses."

—Nigel Phelps

Above: Seismograph illustration with top view by Sean Samuels. Right: Illustration of the automated crossbow by Henry Fong.

Anne Kuljian did another really great job with this set. There were about 500 soldiers and cavalry in that set, all with various bronze weapons and shields. There were four chariots and, I think, sixteen cavalry horses with bronze bridalry. We also sculpted twenty different heads to help achieve the effect that every single soldier was individually cast."

—NIGEL PHELPS

Left: Alex enters the tomb and discovers the terra-cotta army. Above: Scale model of the tomb set.

The Real Terra-cotta Army of Xi'an

On March 29, 1974, local farmers were drilling for water just east of Mount Lishan in Xi'an, Shaanxi Province, China, when they stumbled upon one of the greatest archaeological finds of all time: the buried terra-cotta army. Here they found 8,099 warriors, horses, acrobats, and chariots that had been buried for more than 2,200 years.

The army was originally constructed to guard the tomb of Qin Shi Huang Di, who conquered all of China in 221 B.C. and was named the country's very first "emperor." His power was vast.

At the age of ten, he ordered work to begin on his mausoleum, which was to be guarded by the terra-cotta army. To complete the terra-cotta army, more than 700,000 conscripted laborers worked for almost forty years.

Each warrior is utterly unique with a delicately carved face and individual hairstyle. The faces show the various ethnic groups that made up the army at that time. The taller warriors (over six feet) head the formation. They are the vanguards. Behind them, officers ride horse-drawn bronze chariots. The rest of the army make up the rear formation. Ten partitioning walls separate the warriors into military columns.

It appears that the emperor planned to conquer the after-life riding his chariot. However, in this life, his dynasty died with him. Shortly after his death in 210 B.C., his Qin Dynasty was overthrown. Rebel chief Xiang Yu set fire to the terra-cotta army and destroyed the wooden structures that housed them.

The actual tomb of the Emperor Qin Shi Huang Di, guarded by his terra-cotta army, is believed to house untold gems; it has yet to be opened.

Above and left: Images of the terra-cotta army in Xi'an.

The Terra-cotta Warriors

The terra-cotta warriors of Xi'an are among the most exciting and innovative elements of the movie. As part of the excavation discovered by Alex O'Connell, they were meant to be accurate representations of the actual statues. "When I did the research into the real terra-cotta warriors I saw that they are all in ranks of four," recalls Nigel Phelps. "I'd imagined they were little people, but another surprise was that they are six feet tall and every one is different."

Set decorator Anne Kuljian impressed everyone with her remarkable attention to the detail. "We bought one kind of soldier and horse in China, and then we mass-produced them in a workshop in Montreal," she explains. "I had all the weapons, the armor, and the other items that were needed, like the bridles on the horses and the ornaments in the mausoleum, made by a Chinese team headed by prop master Chung Wai and then shipped to Montreal."

Everything down to the weaponry is accurate to the period. "One of the most exciting things about the terra-cotta warriors is that we've re-created all of the weapons that were stolen hundreds of years ago," explains Phelps. "There were some incredible documentaries on the Discovery Channel and the History Channel that were all about ancient Chinese weaponry, which were a fantastic help!"

Above: Concept illustration by Christian Robert de Massy.

32D). ALEX POURS WATER INTO COMPASS BOWL WILSON WATCHES

33. NEEDLE RISES AS
WATER POURS IN   CUT TO

                                                  CUT TO

36. SINGLE ON WILSON— IS IT WORKING?—   CUT TO

34. ALEX EXPLAINS HOW TO SOLVE
PUZZLE   CUT TO

37. C.U FLOOR SPLITS OPEN UNDER ALEX'S FOOT
                                        CUT TO

35. ALEX AND WILSON FIND TRUE NORTH, ALEX ROTATES STONE COMPASS

Opposite page: Concept drawing of the stone compass by Henry Fong. Set photo of David Calder (Roger Wilson) and Luke Ford (Alex O'Connell) unlocking the compass to gain entry to the inner sanctum of the mausoleum. *Above:* Storyboard drawings of the stone compass scene by Martin L. Mercer. *Below:* Concept drawing of Chinese compass that unlocks the entrance to the Emperor's tomb by Henry Fong.

fact or fiction?

In doing research, I discovered some amazing facts about the Emperor's actual tomb. For example, they've only uncovered a tiny fraction of the warriors buried underground.

"The tomb of the Emperor himself won't be uncovered for another fifty years, even though they know exactly where he is. This is because, by then, they hope to have the technology to do a proper excavation of the site doing the minimal amount of damage.

"There are records that describe the actual crypt that the authorities believe are true. The Emperor's sarcophagus is supposedly placed in the middle of a gigantic miniature model of China, where the rivers flow with liquid mercury—the gas of which would instantaneously kill a tomb raider.

"Supposedly, there are hidden crossbow triggers

everywhere and the ceiling is encrusted with diamonds in the configuration of Chinese constellations. Archaeologists recently did soil tests that did confirm traces of mercury, so they're taking the description very seriously." —NIGEL PHELPS

Above: Concept drawing by Christian Robert de Massy. Opposite: Storyboard panel by Martin L. Mercer. Right: Isabella Leong (Lin) guards the mausoleum from tomb raiders.

Above: Interior concept illustration of the Imhoteps bar by Christian Robert de Massy. Below: The final exterior set.

Right: Costume illustration of Imhoteps dancers by Phillip Boutte, and the final costumes worn by the dancers.

Imhoteps

The Imhoteps bar set was important in a couple of different ways. Firstly, the page count was huge, so it became quite an important pivotal environment. There needed to be enough nooks and crannies to it so we could keep returning there in the story and see different aspects each time.

"Secondly, as a tonal piece, this environment had to represent the kind of place you could've imagined in Shanghai in the 1940s. It needed to be a fun, boisterous place, with a multicultural mix of people.

"This was a great opportunity to give a nod to the previous *Mummy* films with respect to the Egyptian theme. It was a natural direction, given that 'Shanghai deco' took a lot of its inspiration from ancient Egypt. I gave it a bit of a 'moderne twist' to make it a bit more glamorous.

"Anne Kuljian did another great job here with all the tables, chairs, and light fixtures; everything was beautifully custom-made specifically for this set."

—Nigel Phelps

Below: Nightlife, Shanghai-style, 1946. John Hannah (Evelyn's brother Jonathan) shares a martini with "The Princess" (Marcia Nasatir) in the Imhoteps bar.

The Shanghai Museum

I started designing the Museum Rotunda set before I came out to Shanghai to find locations for the exterior. I was trying to imagine what a postwar museum would look like in 1946, and felt it should look like one of those great colonial-style buildings that exist on The Bund in Shanghai, but with more emphasis of a Chinese accent to the architecture.

"I found a great-looking building in Shanghai that was this very imposing Stalinist-type structure. Even though it's a few years incorrect, I felt there were more than enough angles on the place that could be photographed without giving the period away. The architectural style and colors became the basis for the interior set, along with details of the window and column styles.

"However, before too long, it became apparent that the location wanted to charge us so much money that it was cheaper for us to build the exterior entrance as part of our composite set on the back-lot of Shanghai Film Studios, so that's what we did."

—Nigel Phelps

To create a set, designers look at actual buildings and thousands of photographs for inspiration. The exterior of the Shanghai Museum set evolved from an actual state building into the designer's rendition of such an architectural space (left).

Left and above: Illustrations by Christian Robert de Massy.
Right and below: Illustrations by Meinert Hansen.

The Museum Rotunda

The Shanghai Museum Rotunda set was the first to be built on Stage at Mel's Cité du Cinéma in Montreal. "An interesting aspect to the museum set was that there was a stunt that needed to be coordinated on it," explains Nigel Phelps. We had to design a way into the space for Alex and Lin to arrive without being seen. That was a hard set to design because

Opposite above: Concept illustration of the Museum Rotunda by Meinert Hansen. Opposite below: The Rotunda set. Illustration by Christian Robert de Massy. Right: Actress Isabella Leong, in her Matrix-inspired long coat for this scene.

we had to incorporate all of that and the chariot had yet to be designed, so we were pulling and stretching and re-shaping everything to accommodate all the other aspects."

An early draft of the story included a huge museum re-opening party that coincided with Chinese New Year festivities. There was to be a banquet and dancing in and around the entrance lobby, in addition to the exterior museum grounds. In the process of refining the story, Rob Cohen decided those scenes weren't necessary and he chose to focus on the primary reason for being in the museum— this is where the chariot and other relics from the

Emperor's tomb were being unpacked and restored.

To accommodate the action, the set was divided into several different stations exemplifying the restoration process. Cleaning and restoring in one area, documenting

and cataloguing in another, all these different places told a background story. Jean-Pierre Paquet, the art director on this set, integrated the design to match the exterior location in Shanghai.

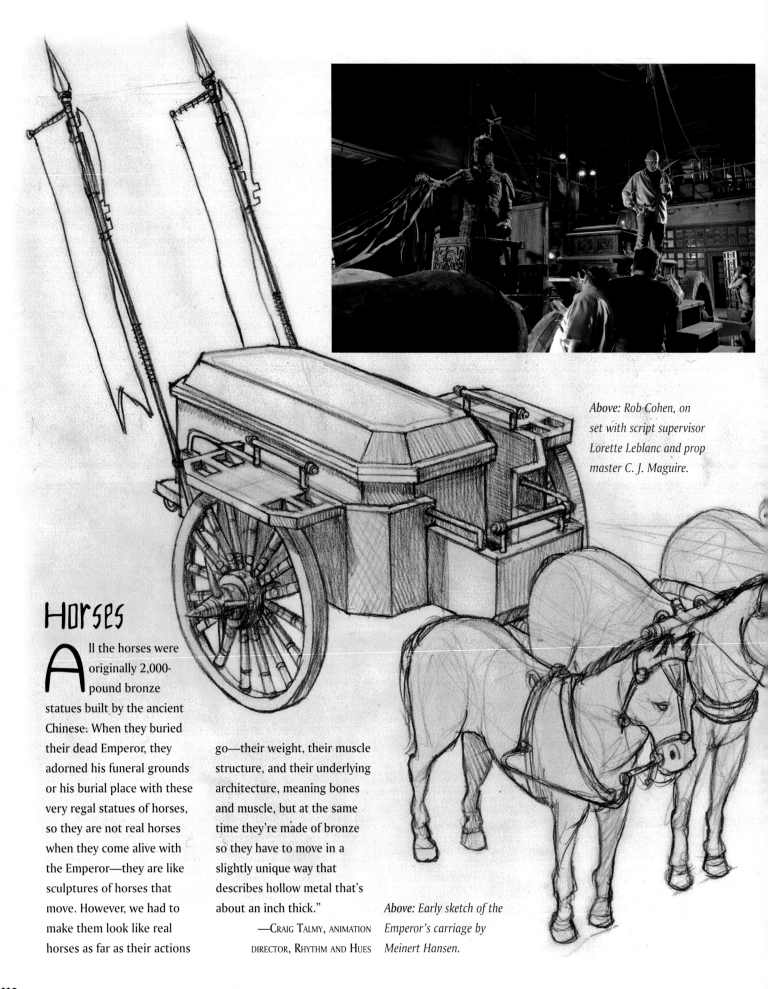

Above: Rob Cohen, on set with script supervisor Lorette Leblanc and prop master C. J. Maguire.

Horses

All the horses were originally 2,000-pound bronze statues built by the ancient Chinese: When they buried their dead Emperor, they adorned his funeral grounds or his burial place with these very regal statues of horses, so they are not real horses when they come alive with the Emperor—they are like sculptures of horses that move. However, we had to make them look like real horses as far as their actions go—their weight, their muscle structure, and their underlying architecture, meaning bones and muscle, but at the same time they're made of bronze so they have to move in a slightly unique way that describes hollow metal that's about an inch thick."

—CRAIG TALMY, ANIMATION DIRECTOR, RHYTHM AND HUES

Above: Early sketch of the Emperor's carriage by Meinert Hansen.

110

The Emperor's chariot went through many design incarnations and ultimately combined the idea of a Hindu funeral cart with that of a gun carriage. *Above: Chariot concept by Meinert Hansen.* **Right:** *Illustration by Matt Codd.* **Below:** *Overhead view of a scale model of the chariot.*

The Emperor's Chariot

The Emperor's bronze chariot was the centerpiece of the Shanghai Museum set. This was one of the first pieces that needed to be designed, because the director wanted to start storyboarding it as soon as possible.

As a basis for the design of the chariot, Rob Cohen suggested using the principle of a gun carriage. Working with concept artist Matt Codd, the department came up with a design that incorporated ancient Chinese imagery with Hindu funeral carts and gun carriages.

Though the design of the chariot had to meet with the director's criteria, it also had to meet the requirements of several departments. SFX had to build it, which altered some things; stuntmen had to drive it; then as ideas and the action got refined, the designers had to modify it to suit other needs too. As a result, the chariot was constantly evolving throughout the production. "There were so many people to please with the design criteria that it became a really difficult object to resolve," explains Nigel Phelps.

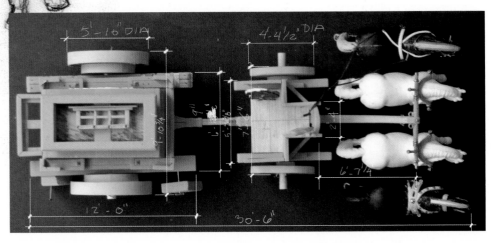

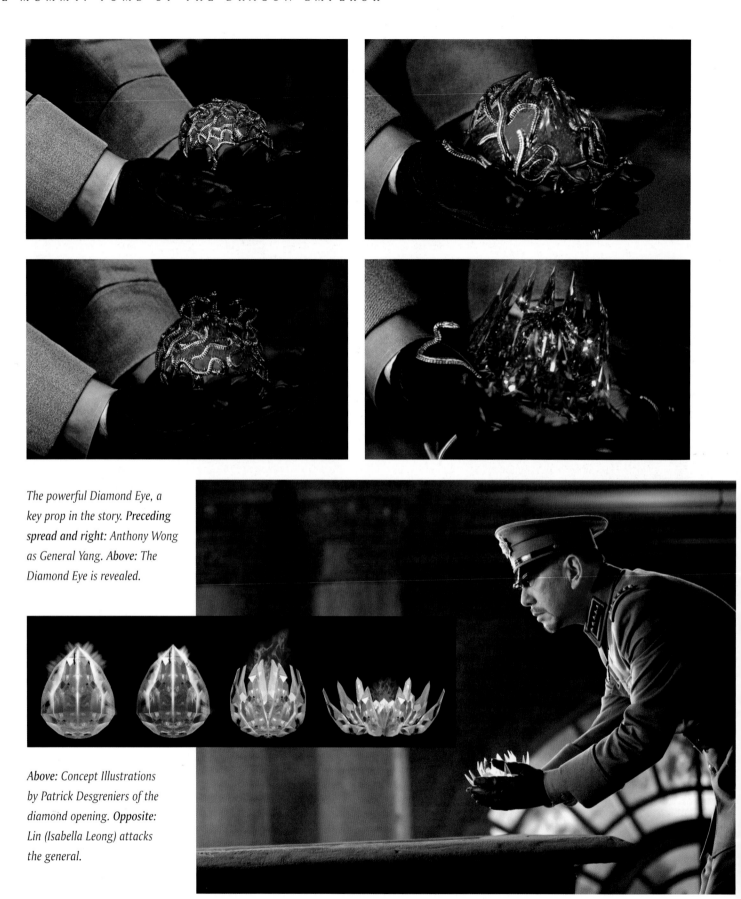

The powerful Diamond Eye, a key prop in the story. **Preceding spread and right:** Anthony Wong as General Yang. **Above:** The Diamond Eye is revealed.

Above: Concept Illustrations by Patrick Desgreniers of the diamond opening. **Opposite:** Lin (Isabella Leong) attacks the general.

The Streets of Shanghai

The Shanghai street sets were created at the Chedun Film Studio, in the Songjiang District outside of Shanghai. The studio already contained an amazing network of sets that re-created the streets of 1900s Shanghai. "When we first began researching what Shanghai looked like in 1946, I was amazed at how much it looked like Las Vegas," marvels Nigel Phelps. "It looked so modern, I thought the dates were wrong. In actuality neon had been around 20 years before then. An interesting thing with the street lighting was that it always felt kind of contemporary until you put an amber wash over everything, then you were instantly back in time.

"One of the main considerations in designing the Shanghai street set was the ability to facilitate both Rob and the action director Vic Armstrong," adds Phelps. "Both have a very energetic

camera style, so we had an army of art department personnel standing by so we could change the look of any street instantaneously. I designed it so that you could turn sections of lights on and off to give a different look. We also had large pieces of scenery and light fixtures that were mobile and could be easily wheeled into place.

"When shooting a chase scene you can easily spend

Various interpretations of the streets of Shanghai in the 1940s, as drawn by Christian Robert de Massy. **Right:** *The set at night.*

too much time and energy on things only to find that you can barely see them because they are passing by so quickly. The ends of the streets were the most important thing, and I made sure we had several different ways of finishing them. We have five streets for the chase—Flower Street, Billboard Street, Bar/Red Light Street, Museum Street, Market Street, and finally the Chinese Opera. We connected them all so the chariot and the fireworks truck could keep turning over indefinitely, going from one street to the next."

Above: The Shanghai street scene before the chase. Below: Dressing the set for the aftermath of the chase through the flower market. *Opposite: Brendan Fraser on a trolley that will transform into* one of the bronze horses through the magic of computer graphics.

The Chariot Chase

The sequence was shot at night and, between the main unit and action unit work, took over three weeks to complete.

"In screen time it's a nonstop chase for seven or eight minutes," says executive producer Chris Brigham. "With every draft that Rob wrote there was a larger explosion, another vehicle. It just got bigger and bigger,

CON'T WIDGNING – DEBRIS SETTLES

–SSC – 6' MUMMY EMPEROR STEPS OUT OF THE (SWELL) STATUE

which at the time made my life more difficult but at the end of the day made for a very exciting and memorable scene."

Although the chariot chase scene was extremely complicated for everyone on set, Rob Cohen recalls filming at least part of it with great glee. "Vic Armstrong, our action unit director, blew up a trolley on the main street in the Shanghai Bund section," says Cohen. "Rick and Jonathan take the mother of all rockets and aim it right at the fleeing chariot. Jonathan lights the fuse with his Dunhill lighter and the rocket rips down the boulevard. The

Mummy deflects the rocket straight into the trolley.

"Vic and I had set up eight cameras and the damn trolley blew ten feet straight up into the air with a fireworks display that could be seen from outer space!

"SFX Supervisor Bruce Steinheimer had designed the event with a team of American and Chinese fireworks experts. The concussion was so intense that it broke every window in the street, and the rocket's red glare set the third story of the set on fire.

"It was glorious!"

Storyboard art by Nikita Knatz.

SSC – THE CHARIOT SIDE-SWIPES THE BENTLEY...

SHANGN / BACKLOT

LEADING SHOT; LOW UP L: EMPEROR CUTS HARD CAM. R...
... YANG NEARLY DECAPITATED BY BIG BUBBA ROCKET
MISSES THE CHARIOT...

SADB → SHOTS

SSC – STAY WITH THE CORTEGE'S SPARE WHEEL AS IT COMES
TOWARD CAMERA, GRINDING SPARKS AS IT 'KEYS' THE
BENTLEY'S PORT SIDE... CUT/WIPE AS THE CHARIOT
PULLS OFF. OS...

SHANGHAI / BACK LOT

(SPARKS FROM HORSES'
HOOVES, CHARIOT WHEELS, ETC)

L ON REAR OF CHARIOT AS IT VEERS
OFF TO THE LEFT... ALEX + LIN UNDERNEATH...

JONATHAN'S POV:
"FRENCH CONNECTION" SHOT

"BACKLOT SHANGHAI"

MOVING POV...

—WIDE SHOT – FIREWORKS ?FROM RUINED TROLLEY?, ETC
(FINAL OF PROGRESSIVE BLASTS FROM BIG BUBBA)

INTRODUCE A TROLLEY
BACKLOT SHANGHAI

REVERSE: JONATHAN MISSES/AVERTS
THE FRIEDKIN BABY CARRIAGE, CAREENS
TOWARD RIKSHAS PARKED IN FG...

45

"SILHOUETTED BY THE AWESOME DISPLAY, THE EMPEROR
WHIPS HIS HORSES AWAY"

121

Storyboard art by Nikita Knatz.

NEW 13
PLEASE REPLACE OLD ONE

LL FP EVY, RICK + EMPEROR ON THEIR HEELS...
("WELL DONE MY LOVE...) RICK GOES BACK

47

LOW MOVING UP L: RICK + HORSE ABOUT TO MEET.

STROBING BG

52

WITH ONE GIGANTIC EFFORT, ETC., RICK ENDS UP ON THE HORSE'S BACK..
(? HORSES + CHARIOT 'TRAVEL' ON BED OF SPARKS'?)

TRACKING SHOT: YANG~ IN THE CHARIOT PART~ IS THROWN BACK, &
ALL HIS SHOTS GO WILD... (NOTE: CHARIOT & SARCOPHAGUS
SWING AWAY FROM EACH OTHER)

LOW UP L~ RICK CUTS HARNESS, REINS..

SEVERAL DETAIL INSERTS

L FROM BEHIND AS THE
SEVERED GEAR SNAPS BACK OS...

LEADING SHOT

RICK SEES THE CHARIOT SARCOPHAGUS
WEAVING BEHIND HIM..

SSC CLOSER TAKES OUT
AND FLIPS OPEN
HIS BUTTERFLY...

LEADING SHOT: RICK PULLS AWAY... DROPS BACK...

The chariot has to interact with the surroundings as if it was being pulled by horses," says SFX supervisor Bruce Steinheimer. "We put a plow on the front of it so we can crash into things because the terra-cotta Emperor and the bronze horses are digital. Their chariot separates and starts to spin out of control. To create that effect, we used a hydraulic spin rig that travels down a track. It ejects the sarcophagus, which slides through the streets causing mayhem and destruction."

After all the crashing through walls was completed, a plastic horse was attached to the front of the chariot. "This gave our actors something to ride on," explains visual effects supervisor Derek Spears. "We replaced the plastic horse with our CG bronze horse later."

Storyboard art by Nikita Knatz.

The Vehicles

Finding vehicles for the film proved to be a huge ordeal when the filmmakers discovered that in the whole of China there are only about twenty period cars and trucks that could be rented for filming. "It really seemed unbelievable to us that there were so few vehicles in a country this size," says Nigel Phelps. "I was convinced it was a mistake or a communication error." But it soon became apparent that this was no mistake.

The solution came in the form of Joe Chi from Hong Kong, who built all of the action vehicles needed for the script from scratch. This included three Chinese army stunt jeeps, two '20s-style fireworks delivery trucks, a copy of a 1948 Rolls-Royce limo that gets sliced in half by a runaway chariot, and a series of mechanized chariot pieces that needed to be manufactured to perform some very demanding stuntwork.

Right: Concept for the fireworks truck by Henry Fong.

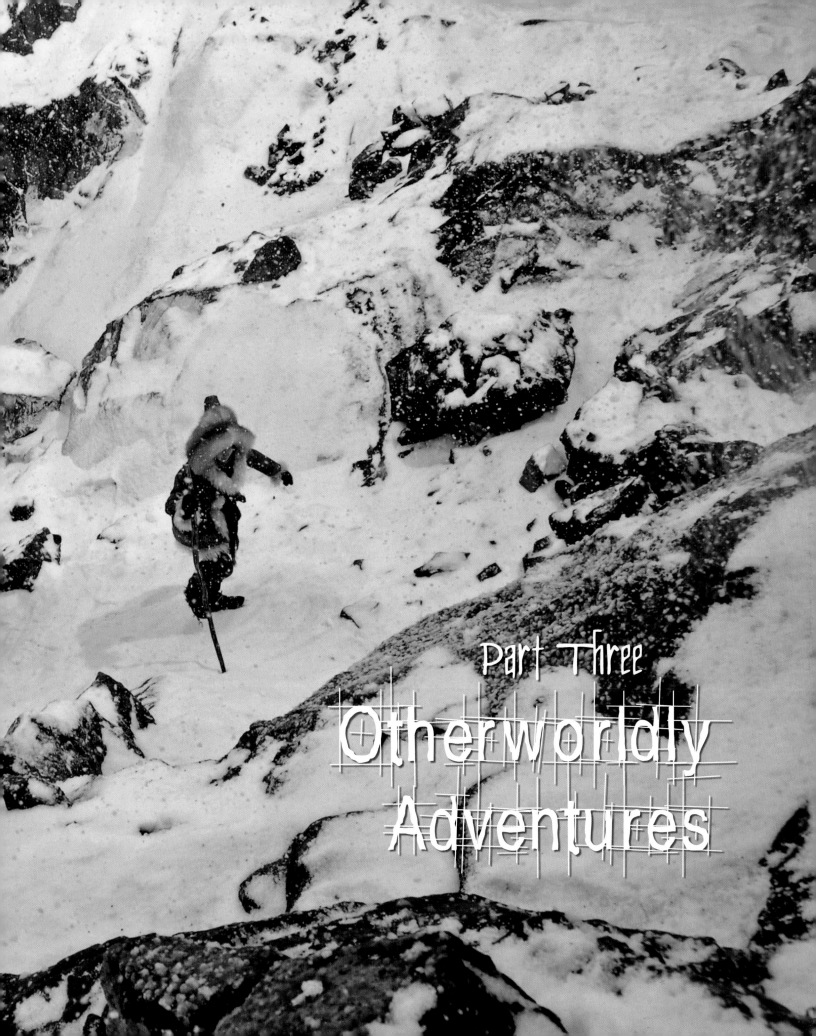

Part Three

Otherworldly
Adventures

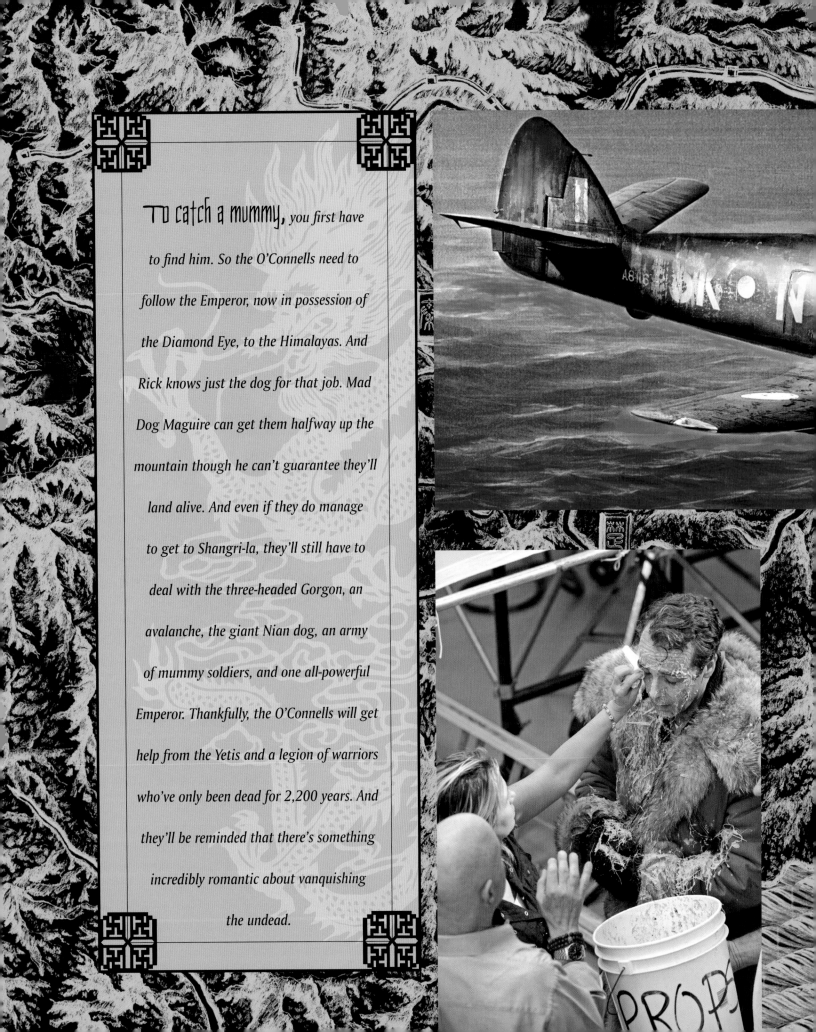

To catch a mummy, you first have to find him. So the O'Connells need to follow the Emperor, now in possession of the Diamond Eye, to the Himalayas. And Rick knows just the dog for that job. Mad Dog Maguire can get them halfway up the mountain though he can't guarantee they'll land alive. And even if they do manage to get to Shangri-la, they'll still have to deal with the three-headed Gorgon, an avalanche, the giant Nian dog, an army of mummy soldiers, and one all-powerful Emperor. Thankfully, the O'Connells will get help from the Yetis and a legion of warriors who've only been dead for 2,200 years. And they'll be reminded that there's something incredibly romantic about vanquishing the undead.

Previous spread: Photo by Simon Duggan. Above: Illustration of Mad Dog Maguire's plane by Patrick Desgreniers. Below left: Actor John Hannah getting slathered in the Yak's yak. Below: Shooting the plane ride on set. Right: Storyboards by Marie-Agnes Reeves of the Himalaya crash.

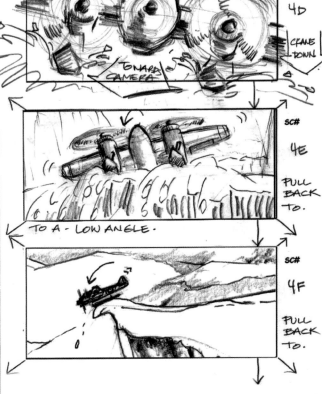

The Gateway to Shangri-la

Rob had a pretty clear direction as to where I should start designing with the gateway to Shangri-la. He described it as being like the lost city of Petra, but here we have a gateway as an opening in an impenetrable wall. You wouldn't see this opening ordinarily. There is a reason why nobody has stumbled across it. You would have to be standing in exactly the right place and the right time in order to see it.

"In Jordan, Petra is carved directly into the rock landscape. I took that idea and made the vocabulary more akin to what you'd expect in China; we ended up with a kind of hybrid of Tibetan, Chinese, and Indian influences.

"The scale is important because it is a huge cliff face with huge columns and steps carved directly into it, and a dramatic icy backdrop beyond. It's an impressive opening that funnels through to a little doorway, which then opens you up into this valley where the courtyard and the golden Stupa are the focal point." —NIGEL PHELPS

Above: Drawing of the rope bridge by Meinert Hansen.
Below: Early sketch of the gateway by Nigel Phelps.

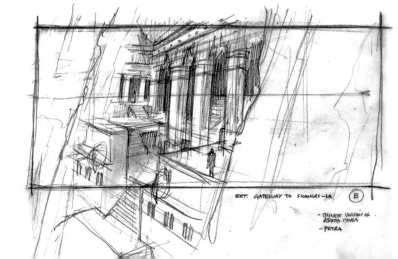

Left: Concept illustrations of the gateway bridge by Patrick Desgreniers. Right: Scale model of the bridge. Below right: Composition matte illustration by Meinert Hansen. Below left: Development illustration of the Stupa at the end of the bridge. Bottom: The finished bridge set in Montreal, Canada.

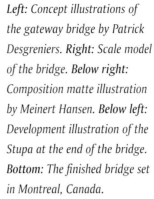

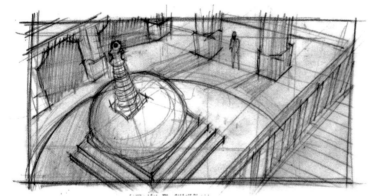

The rope bridge was a particularly nice detail on the Shangri-la set. It was to be in the foreground for much of the scene, so it demanded particular attention. Art director Nicolas Lepage and prop maker Jennifer Small spent weeks researching and testing all different materials to make up the beautifully decrepit-looking Rope Bridge, and the end result looked gorgeous." —NIGEL PHELPS

The Stupa Courtyard

The Stupa Court-yard was meant to look like a haven of tranquillity. (A *stupa* is a Buddhist mound-like structure.) Rob had the idea of using *thangkas* (pronounced "tonkas") to decorate the courtyard. A *thangka* is a painted or embroidered Buddhist banner or scroll painting, which is hung in a monastery or a family altar and occasionally carried by monks in cere-monial processions. In addition to the *thangkas*, the set was decorated with prayer wheels and prayer flags.

Since it is meant to be located in the Himalayan Mountains, the courtyard was dressed with fake snow, the responsibility of SFX supervisor Bruce Steinheimer. "Rob was very specific on the snow he wanted," explains Steinheimer. "We used about 160 tons of magnesium sulfate for the snow on the ground."

Above: Concept drawing of the Stupa temple by Sean Samuels. Below: The Stupa courtyard set. Photo by Simon Duggan.

134

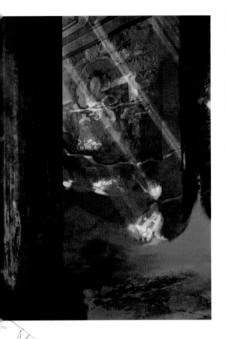

Above: Concept drawing of the snow-covered Stupa Courtyard by Sean Samuels. *Left:* Thumbnail sketch of the Stupa set by Scott Zuber. *Right:* The Stupa-Diamond Eye connection illustration by Henry Fong. *Below:* Concept drawing of the Diamond Eye pointing the way to Shangri-la by Sean Samuels. *Following spread:* Action photos of the actors at work on the Stupa set.

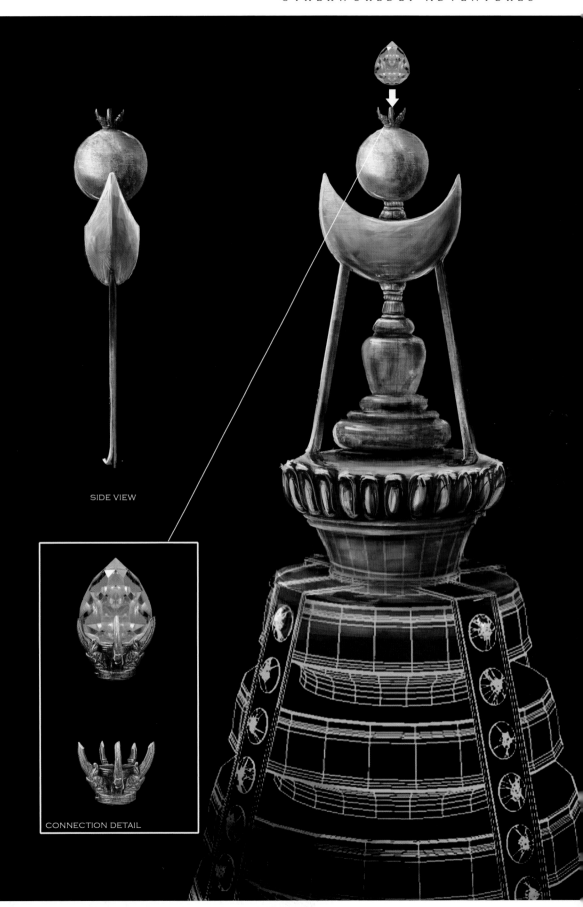

SIDE VIEW

CONNECTION DETAIL

Left: Final Yeti drawing. Above and below: Early concepts for the Yeti. All art by The Aaron Sims Company.

She Speaks Yeti!

For director Rob Cohen, the key to creature design is the logical viability of the creature itself. Could this thing run, fly, and talk? Does its anatomy have logic to it? Can we relate to it from the millions of designs nature has shown us? "I always start with nature," says Cohen. "My first thoughts about the Yeti, a creature who supposedly lives in the cold extremity of the high Himalayas, were: if they did exist, maybe they'd be a mutation of the polar bear. So we began to study the fur, proportions, claws, and biomechanics of that magnificent animal. Later in the process, to increase the 'fierceness' quotient, we turned to the snow leopard, a creature of rare and true Himalayan beauty. The result was a nine-foot tall, white-furred, blue-eyed biped, capable of language, ferocity, action, and humor. We combined the bulk and power of the polar bear with the exotic beauty of the snow leopard, mixed with lots of the art of Aaron Sims."

Animating that art was the job of Craig Talmy, the animation director at Rhythm and Hues. "Our Yeti are Abominable Snowmen—scary as can be—but they're actually friendly and have a good sense of humor," explains Talmy. "Rob wanted them to have different personalities, and as they don't have any dialogue, that needed to read in body language (their furry faces looked pretty much the same).

"For instance, we have one that is more intellectual. He'll run down the hill really fast, and we do a close-up of his eyes that are razor-

sharp, looking at his victim. He stops, looks; we see his thinking process going on and then he smashes the guy in the head. Then the next time we'll have another guy and the same performance is required of him, but what we have is the bumbling guy. He's looking around, preoccupied by everything, not really focused on his task. When he confronts the human, he swings at him in a way that is just sort of accidental, like he almost trips and falls."

To create the individual Yeti personalities, Talmy referenced his high-school days. "I visualized them as being like the football stars in high school or college, but they are not mean-spirited or bullies; they don't go out looking for trouble," Talmy continues. "They're just a bunch of big, fun guys who like to drink beer, party a lot, and high-five each other, but if someone tries to mess with them, they're intrepid. They work together as a team."

Left: Isabella Leong speaking Yeti. Above: The Yeti in a scene from the film.

ALEX FLINGS THE BOMB...

...SENDS THUNDERING REVERBERATIONS THROUGHOUT THE RANGE.

THE EMPEROR HURLS HIS SWORD...

RICK PUSHES HIM OUT OF THE WAY. THE BLADE SLICES THROUGH HIS BACK RIB CAGE...

RICK COLLAPSES...

THE BOMB EXPLODES IN MIDAIR AND...

...FACE DOWN IN THE SNOW... ...THE EMPEROR RETRACTS THE SWORD...

...INTO HIS HAND.

The snow-covered gateway to Shangri-la. **Opposite top:** *The Yeti approach.* **Opposite below:** *Before and after the avalanche.*

Below: *The post-avalanche Stupa. Illustrations by Sean Samuels.* **Top:** *Storyboards by Manuel Plank-Jorge.*

The Shangri-la Cave

The Shangri-la cave was inspired by the Ajanta caves near the city of Jalgaon, in Maharashtra, India. There are thirty caves, some of which are *chaitya-grihas*, or monument halls, and the rest are monasteries. Discovered in 1819, these caves feature paintings dating back as early as 200 B.C. These mostly religious paintings depict Buddha, Bodhisattvas, and incidents from the life of Buddha and the Jatakas, the stories describing previous births of the Buddha.

Director Rob Cohen was clear that the essence of the cave design should be Chinese, not Indian, but since they are geographically located in the Himalayas, the production department had some leeway with their design.

The harder design element was the creation of a Shangri-la, since everyone has his or her own ideas of what such a place should look like.

In the end, the set featured some amazing Chinese sculptures. Though the set dressing may look otherworldly, much of the art is based on actual pieces that were researched by the production department.

Above: Concept drawing by Christian Robert de Massy.
Below: Sketch by Meinert Hansen.

Left: Luke Ford and Isabella Leong. *Below:* The final set of the sleeping Buddha with Rob Cohen and Michelle Yeoh.

143

Everyone has a unique conception of what Shangri-la would look like. *Above:* The final matte painting created for the movie by Syd Dutton of Illusion Arts. *Left and opposite:* Early concept illustrations of Shangri-la by Sean Samuels.

145

The Pool of Eternal Life

Above: Illustration by Matt Codd. *Right:* In a crucial scene, Brendan Fraser is carried to the Pool of Eternal Life. *Below:* Scale model of the Pool of Eternal Life set.

Above: The finished scale model of the pavilion that contains the pool. *Opposite:* Photo by Simon Duggan.

Sc. 132 #1/A
The pool courses with energy and ominously begins to swirl.

Sc. 132 #1/B
The Emperor's human face breaks the surface

Sc. 132 #1/C
Then two more faces break the surface

Sc.132 #1/D
Each connected to long, scaly neck joined to a thick, snake-like body

Sc. 132 #1/E
The creature rises, and rises

Sc. 132 #1/F
finally pushing over the stone canopy.

Sc. 132 #1/G
like it was papier-mache.

#1/H

Sc. 132 #1/I
It lets loose a torrent of fire

Sc. 132 #2

Sc. 132 #3
Alex jump behind a ro

Sc. 132 #4
Jonathan an Evy hide beh a Budda

Sc. 132 #7
Alex " Get away from her"

Sc. 132 #8/A
The Gorgpn bats the lad away

Sc. 132 #8/B

Sc. 132 #8/C

Sc. 132 #9/A
Yang runs along side

Sc. 132 #9/B

Sc. 132 #9/C

Sc. 132 #10

Sc. 133 #1/A
The Gorgon slithers out lik a cobra

Sc. 133 #1/B

Sc. 133 #1/C
arcs upward

Sc. 133 #1/D
The wings spre and snap fillin the air

The Gorgon

In addition to his incarnation of the terra-cotta Emperor, Jet Li's character also has the ability to morph into other forms. "We're using Image Matrix to project Jet's performance onto a CG creature," explains Rob Cohen. "It's really incredible! Jet turns into a three-headed Gorgon. I wanted to see three Jet-heads

Opposite: Storyboard art by Francis Back. Above and right: Concept drawings of the three-headed Gorgon by The Aaron Sims Company.

on this serpentine body, spitting fire and snatching the girl and flying away. It's a mixture of Western and Chinese mythology."

For the animators, the task was to combine the right amount of Jet Li with a three-headed dragon. "The Emperor chose his first incarnation to be a 30-foot, three-headed Gorgon," explains digital supervisor Bob Mercier from Rhythm and Hues, "so we had to decide how much the face should look like Jet Li, and how much it should look like a reptile. The Gorgon needed to have the spirit of Jet Li; the Mummy character should somehow come through. It was our goal to give an Asian influence to the Gorgon's face; you can see a ghost of Jet Li there, but it still works as a creature."

Yang's Camp

Although initially we planned to look for 'Yang's Camp' in the Hangdian area where the landscape is much greener, it was by chance that I noticed these amazing-looking caves in the same area where we were going to shoot the battlefield in Tianmo. It just happened to be an abandoned Ming Dynasty village, and it looked great.

"Rob liked it straight away; he really responded to the secretive, tucked-away aspect of it. In certain light you could barely make out the buildings—they would just blend into the rock, as they were all the same color, and then you also have the contemporary 'Taliban' connections, where it's easy to believe a band of rebels like Yang's hiding out in the caves." —Nigel Phelps

Opposite: Jet Li on set. Above: Jessy Meng and Anthony Wong. Right: Yang's Camp set. Photo by John Platt.

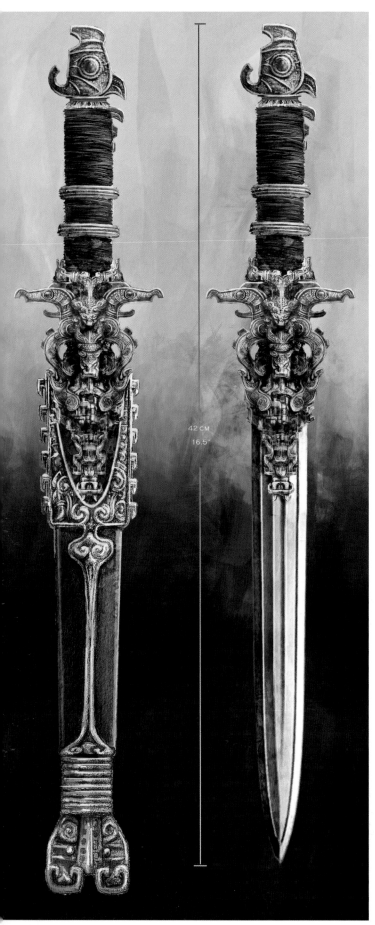

42 CM
16.5"

Left and below: The Dragon
Dagger from 200 B.C. and the
Emperor's swords from 1946,
by Henry Fong. **Opposite above:**
Weapon sketches by Henry Fong
and Yi Zhen Zhou. **Opposite
below:** Concept painting of the
Emperor's helmet by Henry Fong.

JADE INLAY
GOLD PAINT ON LACQUER
CHROME EDGE
CHROME EDGE

Weapons

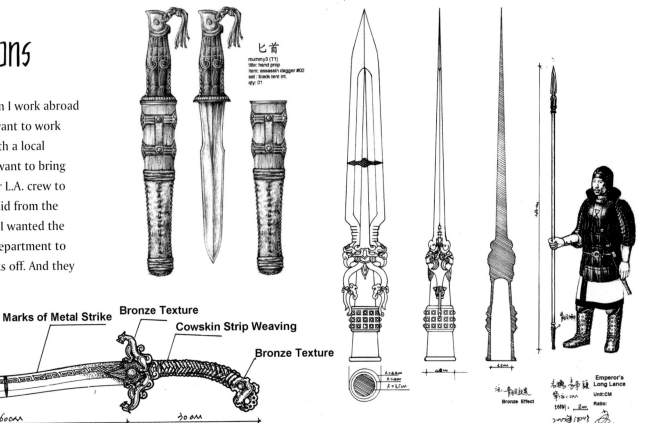

When I work abroad I want to work with a local crew. I don't want to bring my London or L.A. crew to Shanghai. I said from the word go that I wanted the Chinese art department to blow my socks off. And they

匕首
mummy3 (T1)
title: hand prop
item: assassin dagger #02
set : black tent int.
qty: 01

Marks of Metal Strike

Bronze Texture

Cowskin Strip Weaving

Bronze Texture

Emperor's
Long Lance
Unit:CM
Bronze Effect
Ratio:

did. Chung Wai's props are so beautiful because most of them are real. For the 500 figures in the terra-cotta army, the weapons were all made of bronze. All the crossbows had working mechanisms! A lot of things get lost in translation, but no one expected bronze weapons because of the cost. However, in China it was actually cheaper to do it for real than to make them out of fiberglass. It was wonderful because it added another level of believability when the actors touched the swords and they were cold."

—NIGEL PHELPS

The Foundation Chamber

The idea behind the Chamber and the Cog Room was that during the construction of the Great Wall, China's enemies were buried alive in the foundations. The ceiling and walls of the foundation room reflect that. This subterranean world holds all the souls that form the core of the Foundation Army which rises to attack the terra-cotta warriors.

"From my research, I discovered that all over the world, from the beginning of time, man would go back to certain sites time and time again to build a fire

and make offerings to their gods," explains Nigel Phelps. "Fire and smoke seem to be the most primitive basis for anything relating to a religious site. After years and years of consecutive fires, you start to build up and shape the ash, which brings rise to mounds of various shapes and sizes. That's how I designed the subterranean altar. It is fashioned out of ash and dirt, and precedes our story by hundreds of years."

Above and left: Concept drawings of the Foundation Chamber by Christian Robert de Massy. Right: Michelle Yeoh prepares for battle with Jet Li.

Opposite: Jet Li prepares to use the five elements of fire, water, metal, earth, and wood to bring his army to life. Photo by Frank Masi. *Above:* Concept drawing of the altar by Matt Codd. *Left:* Concept drawing of the altar top by Henry Fong. *Below:* Concept drawings of the elements on the altar by Christian Robert de Massy.

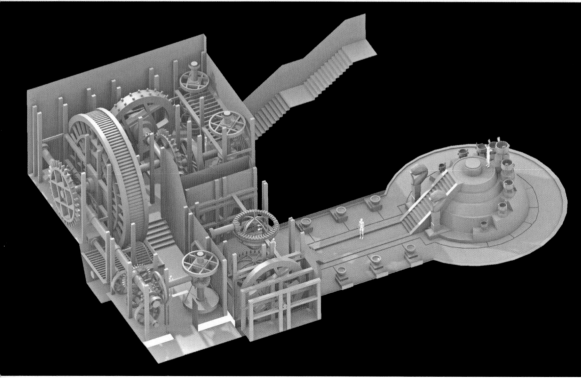

Above: Illustration by Christian Robert de Massy. Left: 3-D rendering of the Cog Room set.

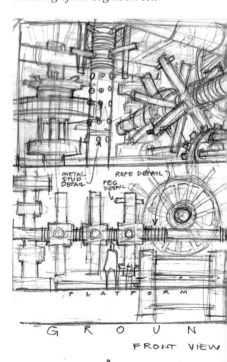

The Cog Room

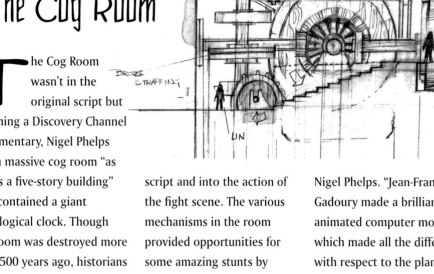

T he Cog Room wasn't in the original script but watching a Discovery Channel documentary, Nigel Phelps saw a massive cog room "as big as a five-story building" that contained a giant astrological clock. Though the room was destroyed more than 500 years ago, historians note that it could tell the position of the sun, the stars, and the month, day, and time.

Director Rob Cohen loved the idea of a gigantic mechanism, so he incorporated it into the script and into the action of the fight scene. The various mechanisms in the room provided opportunities for some amazing stunts by utilizing the revolving 40-foot-diameter wheel and all the other dangerous moving elements.

"This was one of those sets that was impossible to draw beforehand," says Nigel Phelps. "Jean-François Gadoury made a brilliant animated computer model which made all the difference with respect to the planning that went into this extremely technical set."

Above and below left: Sketch of the inner workings of the Cog Room. Below: The final Cog Room set. Photo by Frank Masi.

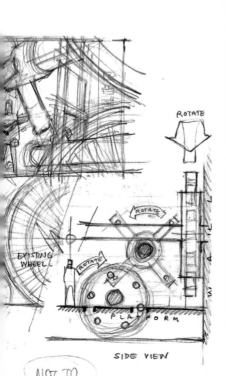

The Battlefield

In order to create the battlefield it was necessary to design something that was graphically recognizable so that you would instantly know which side the terra-cotta warriors were coming from and which way the foundation army were.

"In the west, we had the giant Emperor's bust, which formed the mausoleum entrance where the terra-cotta army lay buried, and in the east we built the dilapidated remains of a much more ancient part of the Great Wall, which is supposed to contain the Foundation Chamber and the Cog Room.

"Before we started to work there, it was just a big empty space that the Chinese army use for tank training exercises. I created the ruins between the two large sets to add interest. A lot of work went into them. They are supposed to be the last remaining vestige of a palace, and they looked very believable." —Nigel Phelps

Opposite: Jet Li on set. Above: the battlefield ruins by Meinert Hansen. Right center: Illustration of arrows in the lintel structure. Right: To-scale illustration of the 1946 battlefield.

TOWER

LINTEL GAG

SUNKEN PIT

1946 BATTLEFIELD
(NOTE: THIS DRAWING IS TO SCALE)

EXCAVATION SITE
(YANG'S CAMP NOT YET INDICATED)

The Legions

Digital Domain was responsible for the creation of the vast armies of both the terra-cotta warriors and the foundation army. Their job was to render 2,500 foundation soldiers and 4,800 terra-cotta warriors.

"The foundation army are the good guys," explains Matthew Butler, co-VFX supervisor. "These are the workers who've been incarcerated under the Great Wall of China for a couple of thousand years. They come to life as these desiccated beings that have a really spooky look. We're not just building them as skeletons, but in a multitude of degraded states, from what we refer to as healthy guys to complete bone men."

The design challenge was to depict a desiccated being as one of the good guys. Searching through somewhat macabre reference books with titles like *The Living Dead*, the animation team built a set of tools that enabled them to create bodies in various states of decomposition, from aged to downright skin and bones.

For the textures the researchers mostly relied on photographic reference, but Joel Hynek, the co-VFX supervisor at Digital Domain, made a useful discovery in his own backyard. "I have a creek in which I found this material that I think is some kind of seaweed. When it dries this stuff looks exactly like mummy skin," he says. "It has a sort of flaky quality and is somewhat fibrous and very organic-looking. We found it very useful in creating the textures we needed."

The terra-cotta warriors also provided their own reference. "We scanned a whole bunch of them, then we came up with cunning ways to swap and exchange body parts so that you never see two that are the same," explains Butler. "We've got a virtual library of geometry of these terra-cotta warriors, together with a virtual library of all the terra-cotta textures. Then you apply the lighting, movement, and the shade of the character to render

Top: Concept illustrations by The Aaron Sims Company of a few of the foundation warriors.

Bottom right: The terra-cotta army crosses the threshold of their tomb.

them. Also, these guys need to break apart. So they have to be modeled in a manner that you could imagine them having locomotion. That's a tricky one because you take what is intrinsically an inanimate object, a stone statue, and build this so it can not only walk around, but do articulate fighting movements."

Nian

Jet Li's character of the mummy Emperor is a shape-shifter who can also control the five elements: earth, fire, air, water, and wood, making him a very dangerous villain. One of his incarnations is the Nian. "The Nian is based on the Foo dog, which was supposed to be a temple guardian. He is half lion and half dog," explains Rob Cohen.

For each of the creatures in the film, Rhythm and Hues produced a 3-D computer-generated model which basically showed muscle tone and skin texture and was sent to the filmmakers for their input. "Once the model is agreed on by everyone, we can move forward and

begin the animation," explains animation director Craig Talmy. "We send it down the pipeline to the rigging department. They are the people who populate the models with all the mechanics to allow it to not just move, but move in the way we want it to."

The Nian is a perfect example of how the initial concept of a creature may have to change in order to make it work for the movie. "The Nian was originally designed to have a man's architecture, a human skeleton in the shape of this

giant dog," explains Talmy. "What we found when you run with that architecture is that human hips aren't conducive to running like a dog. We actually populated it the way we were supposed to, with the right kind of bone and skeletal structure, but it didn't work well. So we went back and ripped out his hipbones, spinal cord, and thighs, and added the underlying structure: the bones and muscles of another creature. We selected a dog, because a dog's hip sockets are very high towards the spinal cord."

In the end, the Nian was a unique creation. "For our version of the Nian, we've taken it into a much more extreme bestial concept," explains Cohen. "It is a very large creature about nine feet high that can grab a plane right out of the skies."

Concept drawings based on a traditional Chinese figure that is half dog and half lion by The Aaron Sims Company. Storyboard art by Francis Back. Following spread: Jet Li and Michelle Yeoh in their climactic sword fight.

169

Storyboard art by Francis Back.

Storyboard art by Francis Back.

About the Filmmakers

Combining nearly three decades of motion picture experience, first as an executive, then as a highly prolific producer, and finally as one of American film's most versatile and successful directors, **ROB COHEN** (Directed by) maintains a unique place in the entertainment industry. In August 2008, Universal Pictures released director Rob Cohen's fourth summer tentpole film, *The Mummy: Tomb of the Dragon Emperor*, starring Brendan Fraser, Jet Li, Maria Bello, John Hannah, and Michelle Yeoh.

His two recent back-to-back blockbusters, *The Fast and the Furious* and *xXx*, proved that Cohen is often on the cutting edge of cultural (pop and otherwise) and technological developments. Those two films have generated over one billion dollars. Cohen's films as both producer and director have swept across a wide range of topics and backdrops, revealing a filmmaker constantly in search of broadening his cinematic horizons.

Cohen's critically acclaimed *The Rat Pack*, an HBO film starring Ray Liotta as Frank Sinatra, Joe Mantegna as Dean Martin, and Don Cheadle as Sammy Davis, Jr., chronicled an entire era as it told the story of Hollywood and Las Vegas' most famous swingers in their heyday. *The Rat Pack* garnered 11 Emmy Award nominations (winning three), won Cheadle a Golden Globe Award, and earned Cohen a nomination from the Directors Guild of America for Outstanding Directorial Achievement in Movies for Television.

Cohen's previous directorial efforts reveal his expansive storytelling interests. His debut film, *A Small Circle of Friends*, starred the late Brad Davis and Karen Allen in a romance set against the political turmoil of late 1960s Harvard University (Cohen's alma mater). Heralded by both critics and audiences, *Dragon: The Bruce Lee Story*—which was both written and directed by Cohen—humanized the legendary Hong Kong–born action hero for new generations, and made stars of both Jason Scott Lee and Lauren Holly.

For *Dragonheart*, visual effects made a quantum leap in Cohen's epic fable of an unlikely alliance in mythical times between a knight (Dennis Quaid) and a fierce but noble dragon endowed with the powers of speech (voiced by Sean Connery). Cohen was intricately involved with both the design of the massive creature and implementation of the state-of-the-art effects from ILM, the first time that a major motion-picture character was fully rendered digitally. The film won the Saturn Award as Best Fantasy Film in 1996, and was nominated for an Academy Award® for Best Visual Effects.

Cohen joined Motown as their executive vice president of the motion picture division while still in his early 20s. At Motown, Cohen produced some key entries in 1970s cinema, several of them antidotes for the "blaxploitation" films of the era. *The Bingo Long Traveling All-Stars & Motor Kings*, starring Billy Dee Williams, James Earl Jones, and Richard Pryor, was a serio-comic look at the "Negro Leagues" of the 1930s. The television movie *Scott Joplin*, which also starred Williams, was the story of the great early-20th-century ragtime pianist and composer. *Mahogany* and *The Wiz* both starred Diana Ross, the former a romantic drama set against the world of high fashion, the latter a screen adaptation of the smash Broadway hit musical. For *The Wiz*, Cohen received the NAACP Image Award for Best Picture, and *Mahogany* received an Oscar® nomination for its now-standard theme song "Theme from *Mahogany* (Do You Know Where You're Going To)."

At Motown, Cohen also produced *Thank God It's Friday*, which was the decade's quintessential disco movie. The film featured superstar diva Donna Summer and such young talents as Jeff Goldblum, Debra Winger, and Terri Nunn (later the lead singer of the group Berlin) at early stages of their careers.

ALFRED GOUGH & MILES MILLAR (Written by) are prolific writer/producers. Their work on *The Mummy: Tomb of the Dragon Emperor* spanned three years, from inception to completion. They collaborated closely with director Rob Cohen to relaunch the incredibly successful *The Mummy* franchise.

Gough and Millar's feature credits include the hit action-comedy *Shanghai Noon*, starring Jackie Chan, Owen Wilson, and Lucy Liu, as well as its sequel, *Shanghai Knights*, directed by David Dobkin (*Wedding Crashers*). Other screenwriting credits include *Spider-Man 2*, starring Tobey Maguire; *Herbie: Fully Loaded*, starring Lindsay Lohan; and

Lethal Weapon 4, starring Mel Gibson and Danny Glover.

Gough and Millar's work also spans the world of television. The duo created and served as executive producers of the critically acclaimed action-adventure series *Smallville*, which is now in its eighth season. *Smallville* is the longest-running comic book–based series of all time and was the #1 show in the history of the WB Network.

SEAN DANIEL (Produced by) has produced *The Mummy*, *The Mummy Returns*, and *The Mummy: Tomb of the Dragon Emperor*. In 1992, he formed Alphaville Productions with partner Jim Jacks. In addition to *The Mummy* series, they produced such films as Richard Linklater's acclaimed *Dazed and Confused;* the renowned western *Tombstone*, starring Kurt Russell; *The Scorpion King;* Nora Ephron's comedy *Michael*, starring John Travolta; *A Simple Plan*, directed by Sam Raimi; the Coen Brothers' *Intolerable Cruelty;* the Chris Rock/Weitz brothers' comedy *Down to Earth;* Jerry Zucker's *Rat Race;* John Woo's first American film, *Hard Target;* William Friedkin's *The Hunted*, starring Tommy Lee Jones and Benicio Del Toro; *The Jackal*, starring Richard Gere and Bruce Willis; and *The Gift*, starring Cate Blanchett and Hilary Swank, also directed by Raimi.

JAMES JACKS (Produced by) was executive producer of the Coen brothers' cult film *Raising Arizona*, before joining Universal Pictures as vice president of acquisitions. During his five years there, Jacks was involved in making such films as *Field of Dreams*, *Do the Right Thing*, *Darkman*, *Jungle Fever*, and *American Me*.

In 1992, he formed Alphaville Productions, one of America's most successful production companies, with partner Sean Daniel.

STEPHEN SOMMERS (Produced by) wrote and directed *The Mummy* and *The Mummy Returns*. He also wrote and produced the spin-off *The Scorpion King*. He wrote and directed *The Adventures of Huck Finn*, starring Elijah Wood and Jason Robards; *The Jungle Book*, starring Jason Scott Lee, Cary Elwes, Sam Neill, and John Cleese; and *Deep Rising*, starring Treat Williams and Famke Janssen. Sommers wrote and executive-produced Disney's *Tom and Huck*, starring Jonathan Taylor Thomas and Brad Renfro.

BOB DUCSAY (Produced by) was one of the original creators of *The Mummy* franchise, having produced and edited *The Mummy* and *The Mummy Returns*.

In 2001, he joined with longtime collaborator Stephen Sommers to form Sommers Company. Universal's release of *Van Helsing* marked their first film under the banner, with Ducsay serving as both producer and editor.

Ducsay's other editing credits with Stephen Sommers as director include *The Adventures of Huck Finn*, *The Jungle Book*, and *Deep Rising*. He also edited *Impostor*, *Star Kid*, and *Love and a .45*.

CHRIS BRIGHAM (Executive Producer) was also the executive producer on *The Good Shepherd*, directed by Robert De Niro; Martin Scorsese's acclaimed film *The Aviator;* and Tribeca Productions' hit comedies *Analyze This* and *Analyze That*, directed by Harold Ramis and starring Robert De Niro and Billy Crystal.

Among other films, Brigham has executive-produced *The Count of Monte Cristo* and *The Legend of Bagger Vance*, and co-produced *Extreme Measures* and *Before and After*. Brigham has worked as unit production manager on *Kiss of Death*, *Six Degrees of Separation*, *Interview with the Vampire: The Vampire Chronicles,* and *Lorenzo's Oil*.

From psychological dramas to heart-pounding sci-fi thrillers, **SIMON DUGGAN**, ACS (Director of Photography) brings his masterful cinematography to every film he shoots. An award-winning member of the Australian Cinematographer's Society, Duggan's feature debut in America was the box-office smash *I, Robot*—his second feature with director Alex Proyas, having previously lensed surprise indie hit *Garage Days*. Duggan's recent feature credits include *Live Free or Die Hard* and *Underworld: Evolution*. Other credits include *The Interview*, *Risk*, and *Guests*.

NIGEL PHELPS (Production Designer) has enjoyed a prodigious career as a production designer. His recent credits include Wolfgang Petersen's *Troy*, Michael Bay's *The Island* and *Pearl Harbor,* and Phillip Noyce's *The Bone Collector*.

Phelps began his career working with Academy

Award®–winner Anton Furst. He started as an illustrator on Neil Jordan's *The Company of Wolves,* and worked as assistant art director on Stanley Kubrick's *Full Metal Jacket.* Phelps next served as art director for Furst on Tim Burton's *Batman.*

Shortly thereafter, Phelps moved to Los Angeles and designed cutting-edge music videos and commercials for a variety of influential directors including Mark Romanek, Alex Proyas, Michael Bay, and Joe Pytka. This work garnered Phelps multiple nominations for MTV Video Awards. His first feature credit as a production designer came on the futuristic science-fiction film *Judge Dredd.* He followed with *Alien: Resurrection* for acclaimed filmmaker Jean-Pierre Jeunet, and he later renewed his collaboration with Neil Jordan on *In Dreams.*

Costume designer **SANJA MILKOVIC HAYS** collaborated with director Rob Cohen for the third time on *The Mummy: Tomb of the Dragon Emperor.* They had previously worked together on *xXx* and *The Fast and the Furious,* also for Universal Pictures. Hays has a diverse roster of other motion pictures that includes *xXx: State of the Union, The Fast and the Furious: Tokyo Drift, 2 Fast 2 Furious, Next, Gridiron Gang, Taxi, Cheaper by the Dozen, Big Fat Liar, Along Came a Spider, Mission to Mars, Star Trek: Insurrection, Blade, 8 Heads in a Duffel Bag, Spaced Invaders, Buried Alive,* and *The Masque of the Red Death.*

She was also assistant costume designer of the fantasy/science fiction films *Mighty Morphin Power Rangers: The Movie* and two smash hits from director Roland Emmerich: *Stargate* and *Independence Day.*

Acknowledgments

Director Rob Cohen would like to thank the following:

Barbara, Kyle, Jasi, Sean and Zoe; Jasin Boland, Marc Pitre; Yi Zhen Zhou, Olympic Lau, Ronnie Shum, Joel Chong, Wong Wai, Pu Zhe Ying, Han Liang, Yi Guang Lei, Joel Chong, Fu De Lin, Christian De Massy, Jack Tung, Sister Xi; Isabelle Guay, Jean-Pierre Paquet, Nicolas Lepage, Réal Proulx, David Gaucher, Meinert Hansen, Sean Samuels, Henry Fong, Patrick Desgreniers, Christian Robert De Massy, Carl Lessard, Alex Touikan, Mario Chabot, Jean-François Fortin Gadour, Martin Gagné, Viorel Indries, Brent Lambert, Céline Lampron, Lucie Paquet, Guy Pigeon, Lucie S. Tremblay; Lyse Pomerleau, Andrée Daneault, Malika Ben Silmane, Micheline Rouillard, Murielle Blouin, Renée Tremblay, Catherine Catou Gelinas, Laurence Lacoste, Valérie Lévesque, Christian Cordella, Philip Boutte, and Russell Shinkle (and his crew).

Publisher Esther Margolis would like to acknowledge the following for their special assistance:

At Universal: Cindy Chang, Daniel McPeek, Jennifer Epper, Angie Sharma, and Bette Einbinder; unit publicist Amanda Brand; associate producer Marc Pitre; costume designer Sanja Hays; Linda Sunshine for her editorial acumen and Tim Shaner at Night and Day Design (nightanddaydesign.biz) for his exciting design; and the Newmarket team, including Keith Hollaman, Frank DeMaio, Paul Sugarman, Heidi Sachner, Harry Burton, and Linda Carbone. And a special note of gratitude to production designer Nigel Phelps for his artistry and insightful comments, and to Rob Cohen for his wonderful introduction and enthusiasm for the book.